WORKING POSITIVELY
WITH TRADE UNIONS

WORKING POSITIVELY
WITH TRADE UNIONS

How to get the best out of your relationship with the trade unions.

The ultimate resource for new or established line managers and HR professionals to develop positive relationships at work. Contains a new concept using a practical Relationship MAP as well as activities, exercises and techniques to maximise your relationship and enhance the organisation.

BERNIE McCARDLE AND TONY WEIGHTMAN

First published 2018

Copyright © Bernie McCardle and Tony Weightman 2018

The right of Bernie McCardle and Tony Weightman to be identified as the authors of this work has been asserted in accordance with the Copyright, Designs & Patents Act 1988.

All rights reserved. No part of this book may be reproduced, stored in a retrieval system, or transmitted in any form or by any means, electronic, electrostatic, magnetic tape, mechanical, photocopying, recording or otherwise, without the written permission of the copyright holder.

Published under licence by Brown Dog Books and
The Self-Publishing Partnership, 7 Green Park Station, Bath BA1 1JB

www.selfpublishingpartnership.co.uk

ISBN printed book: 978-1-78545-356-4
ISBN e-book: 978-1-78545-357-1

Cover design by Kevin Rylands

Printed and bound in the UK

Dedication

We would like to dedicate the book to those people who have supported both of us throughout the process mainly our wives, Susan and Tracey. They have acted as proof readers, mentors and more than anything else have just listened when we needed to off load our progress and ideas.

The inspiration for the book has come from Bernard McCardle Senior who we both know so well. Bernie has to thank him for being a great father and mentor whilst Tony recognises him as a perfect role model for a full-time trade union officer who was true to his word, reliable and professional in his approach. He has offered input and support throughout the process and we could not think of a more worthy person to be associated with in this project.

Contents

1. Introduction	8
2. A brief history of Trade Unions	12
3. Trade Unions and the law	45
4. The MAP and how to succeed	69
5. Building engagement with Trade Unions	97
6. The role of the Line Manager	117
7. Building a positive relationship with the shop steward	147
8. Consultative meetings and process	171
9. The negotiation process	189
10. Discipline and grievance handling	226
11. Shop steward training	253
12. Dealing with difficult situations	268

Appendix

1. How to control nerves — 299
2. Corridor meeting process — 300
3. Grievances Do's and Don't's — 301
4. Disciplinary and grievance phrases — 302
5. McCardle and Weightman MAP — 304
6. MAP Questionnaire — 305
7. MAP Profile — 306
8. Worked example of group mean — 308
9. Major exercises — 309
10. Trade Union Quiz answers — 327

Chapter 1:
Introduction

Managing Trade Unions

In the 1970s and 1980s most line managers and Human Resource professionals had experience of working with trade unions as it was an integral part of day to day working life. Getting the best out of this relationship and keeping the business on course was the territory of a number of skilful people. Such skills are now regarded as almost a forgotten art.

This is mainly due to the fall in trade union membership and a more strict form of employment legislation. This new type of legislation has made it more difficult to take strike action and operate a closed shop. These had been two sacrosanct aspects of trade unionism for many years and had led to more difficult situations for employers who want to make significant changes to the way they work.

In the last fifteen years there has been a level of trade union membership that is lower than for many years and declined significantly from the 1980s before stabilising around 2011. The need for the specialist skills of working with trade unions has been lost as most companies have relied too much on the lawyers and a much less forceful trade union.

In more recent years we have seen more and more line managers and HR professionals having to work in a new type of environment where they need to deal with a more active and in some cases a resurgent trade union. Most of these managers have not been shown or trained in the necessary skills to get positive resolutions whilst developing effective working relationships. The old hands who practised the forgotten art are mainly retired and therefore unable to help or pass on their knowledge.

This book has been designed to fill that knowledge and skill gap. By using real situations we can explore how best to manage trade unions to gain a win/win outcome and drive the organisation forward.

The book draws on the experience of two practitioners who have been actively involved with managing trade unions in different types of organisations. Their experience can be used to act as the missing sounding board that the old hands would have provided.

The book's approach is to focus on long-term relationships rather than try to get short-term gains. With such a focus you can develop a positive non-adversarial approach which will give both parties an opportunity to develop and understand each other's views and perspective on given issues.

You can use this book as a total experience and gain from every chapter. This will cover the history of trade unions through to the different skills that can be applied in specific situations such as pay negotiations or discipline. There is special reference to building effective working relationships which can lead to greater engagement and a better working atmosphere. We have developed a MAP process for use in identifying where your current relationship lies with your trade union. This will assist you in developing a route forward to enhance your joint working relationship.

The area of managing the local shop stewards explores this critical relationship, before looking at areas of working together. These areas include meetings, consultation and dealing with difficult situations. The area of shop steward training will also be addressed.

You can also use the book as a reference source to refer to when required.

In this way you can select the chapters that are relevant to your current situation. There will be a number of checklists, quizzes and diagrams to help relate the content of the book to your workplace. The MAP approach can be applied in any given situation at work and will assist you in developing the long-term relationships you desire. Feel free to use these practical aids and be honest with yourself when using them. In this way you will get the maximum benefit for yourself and the organisation.

We believe this book will help those managers and Human Resource managers who want to be seen as professional in their dealings with trade unions but lack the experience of working in this arena. The practical approach in the book relates to real situations and good working practices. It also uses some common sense approaches and practices which will help the manager use some of their already honed current skills in their dealings with trade unions.

We have attempted to cover all the areas that are relevant to most organisations so that you will be able to relate to the content when looking at your work situation. We may not have all the answers to all of your questions but we have tried to offer a number of approaches that have worked in different organisations. By considering these approaches you will have new alternatives to apply back at your work place. The more options you consider, the better the eventual solution is likely to be.

Take your time to look at each chapter and what it can offer you and your organisation. Try to use an open mind approach to the concepts and look at how you can apply or amend these to fit the situation you face. By using the MAP approach you will be able to track your progress in developing effective working relationships. This will assist you in putting the correct amount of effort into the right areas that matter to your working relationships.

We want you to succeed and go on to feel even more confident when dealing with trade unions. This can be achieved by taking your time to find the right approach and address the correct issues to take you forward together and help you to feel you are making solid progress.

Appendix 9 will contain copies of each of the major exercises. This will allow you to re-run them at a later date. It can also act as a reference of the main points.

Each chapter has a summary of key points at the end. This will act as a great reminder to the casual reader or a confidence boost to the less experienced manager. We hope you enjoy your journey through the world of trade unions. We hope you feel the content is practical enough to assist you in developing even better relationships with your trade union members. Good Luck

Chapter 2:
A Brief History of Trade Unions

Introduction

When you join a new company, you tend to research how they have performed in the past and identify their values and mission. This enhances your knowledge and understanding and makes you more confident about making the decision to join. When you arrive, you will want to know what has gone on in the past so you are aware of the history and what has worked and what has created difficulties. This helps you to settle into the job and allows you to understand why certain things happen. This will make sense to most people as we want to succeed in what we do and be accepted. We want to be accepted as quickly as possible as it helps us to contribute in the right way. For most people this is not difficult.

Our Induction gives us most of this information. We get the rest of the information by asking relevant questions. The same is true for a business when they get a new client. It is essential to quickly understand your client's needs and expectations and to get to know as much as you can about them, their values, their history, etc. It is important to establish they will be able to pay for the goods or services supplied. At the end of the day there is no point in dealing with organisations who cannot pay for what you have delivered.

Building Your Knowledge Base

This sort of research is quite normal and the better our research is the more informed and knowledgeable we become and the better chance our business has to succeed.

We should apply the same approach to dealing with trade unions. Working with trade unions is ultimately about relationships and, as is the case in many relationships, knowledge and understanding are crucial ingredients to establishing and developing the relationship. The better you understand them, and indeed the better they understand you, the better the relationship and the business can flourish.

This aim of this chapter is to provide you with a brief historical context and working understanding of trade unions. It is by no means a history lesson or a detailed academic study but will give you an understanding of the key events that have shaped the trade union movement and explain why they exist and how they are structured.

The satirical film 'Monty Python's Life of Brian' infamously coined the saying 'what have the Romans ever done for us?'

Of course, the legacy of the Romans is still all around us today and just a few examples include:

- Plumbing and sanitation
- Roads
- Town design
- Currency
- The 365 day calendar
- Democratic government

You are probably asking yourself, what is the relevance of this to trade unions? The answer is none, other than to jog our thinking. Just as it is easy to forget, underestimate or take for granted the significance of the Romans on modern civilisation, the same can be true in the case of trade unions in terms of modern-day employment.

So, What Have the Trade Unions Ever Done for Us?

Take 10 to 15 minutes to think about what the trade unions have done to improve modern-day working conditions shared by most workers across the UK today and complete the table below.

Things the trade union have done that have benefited me

-
-
-

Working Positively with Trade Unions

It is not always easy to think about what benefits the trade unions have brought us, as we often take these things for granted and focus on the negative side of the relationship.

The fact is over the last two hundred years trade unions have done a massive amount to improve the working lives of workers across all sectors and industries. It is highly likely that every reader of this book will have benefited, whether they realise it or not, from the collective contributions of trade unions over many decades, past and present.

Beyond their direct impact on the workplace, trade unions have also changed the face of British politics and, through the Labour party which they formed, given a voice in parliament to the working classes. The table below highlights some notable worker benefits that have been brought about by the contribution of trade unions:

> **Benefits the trade unions have brought to modern employment across the UK**
>
> 1. The 5-day working week
> 2. Paid leave
> 3. Protection against excessive working hours
> 4. Work-based pensions
> 5. Improved health and safety
> 6. Access to work-based training
> 7. National minimum wage
> 8. Protection from discrimination in the work place
> 9. Sickness absence benefits
> 10. Protection from unfair dismissal

I would imagine many people will be unaware of the role of trade unions in securing the benefits above. It is generally regarded as a surprise that so much of what we take for granted in our working life has come from trade union campaigning and collective bargaining.

Common Goal

Trade unions understandably want the best for their members and likewise successful businesses (public and private) want the best for their employees i.e. we share a common goal. However, all too often somewhere along the way this common goal seems to become detached.

Let us take a few minutes to think about the barriers that prevent employers and trade unions achieving this common goal of what is best for the business and best for the employees. List the things that inhibit management and trade unions reaching agreement on mutually acceptable terms and conditions for staff. We have split the table below to help you think about trade union barriers e.g. unaffordable pay demands, and likewise to think about potential management barriers e.g. not prepared to train the staff.

Barriers to Achieving this Mutual Success	
Trade Union Barriers	Management Barriers
1.	1.
2.	2.
3.	3.
4.	4.
5.	5.
6.	6.
7.	7.
8.	8.
9.	9.
10.	10.

Working Positively with Trade Unions

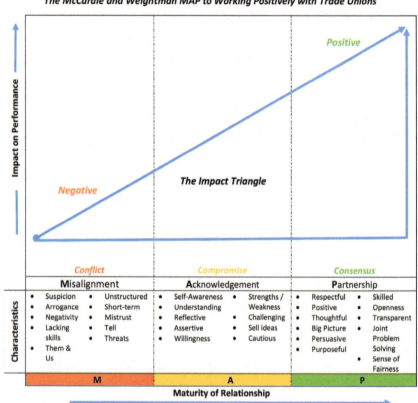

Of course, identifying barriers to success is of limited use unless we do something to address these. To help you do this we have developed a unique model called the MAP and developed several practical tools and techniques to help you identify where you fit against the MAP and to help you establish a route to help you achieve positive, productive and sustainable trade union relations and achieve the goal of mutual success.

The MAP is a unique model developed by the authors that reflects three key stages of maturity in terms of management / trade union relations. It schematically shows that as relations mature, the underpinning tone of the relationship moves from one of conflict to compromise and ultimately consensus. Likewise, as the relationship matures the probability of there being a positive impact on the business increases.

We will give you a detailed overview of the MAP in chapter 4 and how to use it in your own workplace. But before we get to that point, it is important to stress that at the heart of the MAP is your relationship with your trade union and your skill in developing a positive relationship. This relationship will be significantly enhanced by having a sound working knowledge of the history and role of trade unions. The rest of this chapter aims to give you that foundation of knowledge to take forward and reflect on as you progress through the rest of the book and start to use the MAP in your workplace.

Test your knowledge

Let us with start with a short quiz to get you thinking about the history of trade unions. Have a go at answering the following questions. Jot down your answers and reflect on these as you progress through the book.

Question	Your Answer
1. What historical event proved to be a tipping point for the trade union movement?	
2. When were trade unions legalised?	
3. What year was the General Strike?	

Working Positively with Trade Unions

4. What did the General Strike achieve?	
5. What is the main reason people join a trade union?	
6. How many people in employment in the UK are members of a trade union?	
7. Which gender is most likely to be a member of a trade union?	
8. Which occupational group are most likely to join a trade union?	
9. How many registered trade unions are there?	
10. How many strikes were there in 2016?	

Answers to the above questions can be found at Appendix 10

What Do Trade Unions Do?

Trade unions are so much an integral part of the fabric of working life, we pretty much assume what they are there to do and how they function. However, what we have found from working with a large number of managers is that this is not always the case.

Trade unions exist to *protect and promote* the common interest of their members. Their core activities are represented in the diagram below:

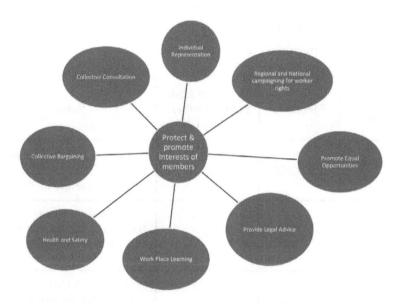

Their core purpose has pretty much remained unchanged, has stood the test of time and is unlikely to change much in the foreseeable future.

How Are They Structured?

Trade unions are the largest example of a voluntary organisation and historically were established to represent the interests of specific groups of workers such as coachbuilders, mechanics, agricultural workers, miners, etc. Some were established to represent the interests of their members in a single organisation such as the Nationwide Group Staff Union for the Nationwide Building Society.

Many trade unions were relatively small with only a few thousand members or less but with the passage of time specific industry-based unions are now less common. Many have gone by the wayside, ceased to exist or are but an insignificant remnant of their formal dominance in the industrial landscape e.g. the National Union of Mineworkers. Today there are about 40 registered trade unions in the UK. Twelve of these trade unions represent over 90% of all trade union members and just three, the big three, represent over 50% of all members (see table below):

Trade union	Members	% of total trade union members in the UK	Notes
Unite the Union	1,424,300	22%	Formed in 2007 by a merger between Amicus and TGWU. UCATT merged in 2017.
UNISON	1,301,500	20%	Formed from merging NALGO, NUPE and COHSE as a union for public services workers.
GMB	613,400	9%	Formed from General, Municipal, Boilermakers and Allied Trade Union, as a general workers' union.
Others	3,187,359	49%	
Total	6,526,559	100%	

These big unions are big businesses and just like any other business they must be economically viable and need to continuously adapt to supply and demand. Individual membership subscriptions, typically £10 to £20 per month, are the greatest source of income for any trade union. The largest trade union, Unite, has an annual income from member's subscriptions of more than £16m. The bottom line is members want something in return for their money and the trade unions need to keep their customers happy i.e. their members, and provide services that are valued. Most members judge the success of their trade union in simple terms e.g. the level of pay rise, increased annual leave, success in defending them in discipline and grievance cases. If they don't deliver, then just like any other businesses, trade unions risk becoming unviable.

All trade unions are structured on a broadly similar model:

National Office	Headed by the most senior trade union official – the General Secretary is the national figurehead normally accountable to the Executive Committee. The General Secretary is supported by their national office and tends to deal with matters of policy, governance of the union, political lobbying and national campaigns
District / Regional Office	Headed by the Regional Secretary and staffed by (paid) full-time union officers (sometimes called Regional Organisers)
Local Branches	Headed by the Branch Secretary. This is normally an unpaid position
Shop Stewards	The term shop steward is an accredited official of the trade union, sometimes called a union or workplace representative and just referred to as the union rep
Union members	Subscribers and life blood of the union

The Union Rule Book

Trade unions have formal constitutions setting out their detailed rules and regulations (colloquially often referred to as the Rule Book) and are structured, as many big businesses are, with clearly defined organisational structures, hierarchies and support functions.

The Rule Book sets out the key policies and procedures for the governance of trade union business, not dissimilar to Company Handbook, Standing Orders and Financial Regulations that most business and organisations have. Trade unions are democratic organisations, accountable to their members (in the same way companies are accountable to their shareholders) for their decisions and conduct. The Rule Book defines who can make what decisions e.g. this might include who determines whether the trade union will support a member's Employment Tribunal case, who can formalise a dispute with an employer, who gets to vote on what, etc. I have recently experienced a very frustrating situation where support of the full-time officer was secured, but he was pretty much powerless, under their Rule Book, to overrule two local shop stewards who were being completely intransigent to a change proposal.

The Shop Steward

For most members, the biggest influence is their local 'rep' or shop steward. This is the person who to them is the face of the union, and the person they will go to if they need any advice or support. Members will often off-load their frustration and displeasure with the company or with a particular work situation onto to the shop steward and expect him or her to communicate this to 'management'. I wish I had a pound for every time I have heard a worker say to the shop steward 'and you can get them (i.e. management) told this or that'.

Similarly, directors off-load their frustration about the trade union on to the line managers or HR and expect them to sort it out with the shop steward(s). There are many excellent shop stewards who have the self-confidence and ability to skilfully quell such frustrations from their members and who are able to filter out many issues before they even get to management.

In these situations, shop stewards are making decisions on which issues are legitimate and have enough justification to raise with management. They recognise that it is not feasible to simply raise every issue that every member has and are actually looking after the interests of the business as well as their members (it is not in the best long-term interest of the trade union just to bombard management with frivolous gripes).

Shop stewards can face a lot of criticism from some members for not taking forward their issues and this important role that shop stewards undertake often goes un-noticed and can be easily overlooked and underestimated by management. It is significantly to management's benefit to help support their shop stewards to get to this stage of self-confidence and ability.

Democracy in Action

Trade unions are organised on democratic principles and many of the roles are subject to periodic elections, meaning the trade union members get to decide who gets appointed. The reality is, as with many elections, lots of people aren't interested in having any active role in their trade union and it is generally the more vocal and visibly active members who put themselves forward to become accredited shop stewards. Shop stewards may not necessarily be the most technically able employees, but they do tend to have great enthusiasm for the role, want to represent their members well and are generally prepared to put a significant amount of their own time into the role. They often have leadership qualities that may not be evident in their day job i.e. the job for which they are employed.

It is not unusual, particularly with less experienced shop stewards, for this energy and enthusiasm to come over as arrogance, threatening, and disrespectful. 'Bolshie' is the term often used to describe such reps. Of course, not all shops stewards could be regarded as bolshie, but even if they are it is important to recognise that they are democratically elected and are therefore the individuals that managers and HR practitioners must then deal with. We will look at this in more detail as we progress through the book.

It should also be noted there are some exceptional shop stewards who are highly capable individuals. Many have gone on to become excellent managers and there is a well-trodden path of trade union shop stewards going on to become successful full-time union officers, HR managers, Members of Parliament, employment lawyers and Employment Tribunal judges.

Many shop stewards establish positions of considerable influence within the union, and indeed within their organisations. They often have a great deal of autonomy within their union, accountable to the union Rule Book and their members, rather than any individual in the trade union hierarchy as would be the case in paid employment. The paid full-time officials are very mindful of the role of the shop steward and whilst they will get involved in more complex cases, the full-time official is first and foremost there to support their shop stewards.

Training and Support for Shop Stewards

It is normal practice that once elected, shop stewards undergo training from their trade union to equip them to undertake their role. The training provided by trade unions is generally of a very high standard and often shop stewards are more highly trained and better equipped in matters of employment law, negotiation skills and matters of discipline and grievance procedures than the managers they are dealing with on a day to day basis.

They often have a greater amount of time (including statutory facility time) to focus on a specific issue or case than the manager who they might be dealing with. This can be incredibly frustrating for the manager and can easily be a source of conflict.

Furthermore, shop stewards have direct access to skilled and experienced full-time officers for more expert advice and support and likewise the full-time officers have direct access to expert legal advice. HR practitioners and managers would be wise not to under-estimate the expertise available to shop stewards and union members e.g. if you end up in an Employment Tribunal it is highly likely you will be up against a skilled employment lawyer, not the local shop steward.

But Where Did It All Start?

For centuries workers have sought to organise themselves and use their collective strength and resolve to protect themselves and stand up against unfair treatment, and to fight for better pay and working conditions. Likewise governments, who were historically controlled by the aristocracy and rich industrialists, have tried to restrict the collective action of workers. As far back as 1800 the Tory government of the day implemented the Combination Act aimed at crushing industrial action by workers.

The Act banned workers from organising themselves or 'combining', to use the phrase of the time. The Act outlawed trade unions (a form of combination), but the effect was simply to drive labour organisations underground and did little to thwart the resolve of workers to seek fair treatment and decent pay. It should be emphasised that many workers at this time were working in the most appalling conditions, living in abject poverty and being exploited to further enhance the wealth and power of their employers.

The Luddites

One of the most notable historical examples of industrial action was the Luddites. The name luddite is derived from a young apprentice called Ned Ludd who was rumoured to have smashed weaving machines. The Luddites were a group of skilled textile workers from Nottingham who, during the early 19th century, rebelled against the introduction of new machinery (modern technology in today's language). The Luddites considered the use of the new machinery, which was becoming more commonplace as the industrial revolution gathered pace, as a way of getting around standard working practices and feared their hard-earned skills would be replaced by machines and unskilled labour.

The Luddites took up their protest in 1811 and this soon escalated into extreme action e.g. breaking into mills and factories, smashing up machinery and even setting premises on fire. It became a very bloody dispute and some mill owners took to shooting protesters dead, and ultimately the Luddites had to be suppressed by military force.

As is often the case with the passage of time, the severity of the conflict gets diminished and today the term Luddite has become synonymous with people who resist change and oppose the introduction of new technology. It is a term often used in a disparaging or negative way without the knowledge of the origins of the term.

It is important to reflect on the scale of poverty many were living in at that time, the fear people would have had of losing their jobs and the deprivation that would follow. These were the toughest of times for the working classes. The significance of this very brief reference to the Luddites is that the technical advancement, and the drive for ever increasing business efficiency is still, 200 years on, at the centre of many modern-day industrial disputes.

This was a period of major industrialisation and political radicalism. Sympathy for the plight of the working classes was growing and after much lobbying the Combination Act of 1800 was repealed within just a few years and replaced with a new Combinations of Workmen Act 1825.

This new Act made some acknowledgement to the combination of workers, either for a one-off purpose such as strike action or in the form of trade unions, but still significantly limited their activities and imposed severe criminal sanctions for picketing and other methods of persuading workers not to work i.e. it made strikes illegal.

However, this did not diminish the collective will of workers to protect their terms and conditions and what happened a decade on would prove to be a seminal moment in the history of trade unionism, and indeed for the future of industrial relations.

The Tipping Point – A Key Moment in History

In 1833 a group of farm workers from the village of Tolpuddle in West Dorset formed the Friendly Society of Agricultural Workers (a trade union) to which members had to swear an oath of secrecy. The union protested against pay cuts being unilaterally imposed by the wealthy farm owners. Their representations to their employer fell on deaf ears and the pay cuts continued. Like the Luddites before, protesting farm workers took to smashing up threshing machinery and burning crops. This was again a bloody dispute and brought severe punishments.

Ultimately six of the trade union leaders were rounded up in the middle of the night, shackled and arrested. They were found guilty of administering 'oaths of secrecy' i.e. to their trade union, and sentenced to transportation to Australia to serve hard labour in the severest of conditions for seven years. However, their sentencing led to an unprecedented, nationwide wave of public outcry and support in favour of the trade union leaders. This was a quite remarkable event, particularly given the limited printed media, no telephones, no television or even radio, never mind social media!

Nonetheless, news of the convictions spread, the strength of public support grew and ultimately this led to their convictions being quashed. The trade union leaders were pardoned and returned home as heroes. They became known as the Tolpuddle Martyrs and have since become enshrined in the history of the trade union movement.

The victory to pardon the Tolpuddle Martyrs confirmed the right of workers to organise themselves into a trade union and it is widely recognised that their story was the inspiration that gave birth to trade unionism as we know it today.

The ability of a small number of men living in abject poverty with little education and suffering exploitation from rich and powerful farm owners, to have the aptitude, endeavour, resilience, vison, integrity and bravery to establish their trade union, fight the cause for their members and consequently suffer the most extreme punishment should never be underestimated. They changed the world of industrial relations forever and set the foundations for fair treatment and work benefits we all enjoy today.

Royal Commission and Legalisation of Trade Unions

The pace of the industrial revolution continued unabated, and with it the growth of trade unions. The collective voice of the workers, combined through their trade unions, was becoming more and more powerful and with this political opinion started to change.

A Royal Commission was established in 1867 by the Tory government of the day to 'Inquire into the Organisation and Rules of Trades Unions and Other Associations'. The Commission concluded that the establishment of trade unions was to the advantage of both employers and workers and the recommendations of the Commission, albeit in the form of a minority report, gained the support of the recently elected Liberal government, under the premiership of William Gladstone, and became enacted through the 1871 Trade Union Act.

This was the Act that legalised trade unions and afforded them the full and positive protection of the law. This Act remained on the statute for over a hundred years, eventually being replaced by the Trade Union Act of 1974.

Trades Union Congress (TUC)

It was just after the Royal Commission that the Trades Union Congress was formed in 1868. Just as individual workers were benefiting from their combined strength and membership of a trade union, it became clear that trade unions could benefit from their collective strength through affiliation, and hence the creation of the TUC. The TUC went on to create the Labour party in 1900 so that working people could have their own representatives in parliament.

The TUC is not a trade union, but brings trade unions together and helps develop common policies on key issues such as the economy, employment law, equality at work, etc. The TUC plays a key role in lobbying government and running campaigns on economic and social issues. Most notably in 1948 the NHS was created because of trade union campaigning (source: tuc.org.uk).

The TUC has played a key role in promoting partnership and assisting unions (and business) to establish partnership agreements and promoting a very different and modern relationship with business. This approach to partnership working is a core principle of the MAP we are going to discuss in detail in chapter 4.

The Rise and Fall

The prominence of trade unions grew rapidly during the latter part of the 19th century and through to the mid-20th century with membership peaking at 13 million in 1979. During this period trade unions were a dominant presence, particularly in the nationalised and heavy industries such as steel, coal mining, docks and engineering. However, since then membership levels have declined sharply, particularly during the 1980s and 1990s, with many attributing this to the impact of the Thatcher government(s) and the reforms she introduced to significantly curb the powers of trade unions. Interestingly, despite a return to a Labour government under the leadership of Tony Blair in 1997, the 'Thatcher' reforms remained in place.

Here to Stay

However, trade union membership has been broadly stable since 2011 and with 6.6 million members there is little doubt that trade unions are here to stay and will continue to be a major part of our employment landscape.

5 KEY FACTS ABOUT TRADE UNION MEMBERSHIP

1. Nearly half of all UK employees work in organisations where a trade union is present. This is as high as 65% in South Yorkshire and 60% in Tyne and Wear.
2. More than half of public-sector employees are a member of a trade union.
3. In the private sector levels are lower at 13.5% but showing some increase.
4. Union membership in workplaces with more than 50 employees has increased to 31%.
5. Women and people employed in professional occupations are more likely to be a member of a trade union. Just over a quarter of all women employees are a member of a trade union.

Source: Figures based on report published by the Department for Business, Energy and Industrial Strategy, 31 May 2018.

It is generally recognised that a core role of a trade union is to secure improvements in the terms and conditions of employment for their members. It has also been widely acknowledged for more than 150 years that trade unions are good for workers, business and the wider economy. Trade unions play an important role in ensuring a fair balance of power and distribution of wealth for workers in terms of the income they help generate. The diagram below highlights the varying forces that can so easily tip the Scales of Power out of equilibrium.

The Scales of Power

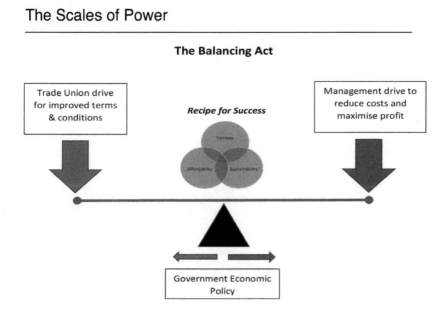

Achieving this balance is a delicate one. Delivering the Recipe for Success can be a challenge for the employers and trade unions. This can be made even more complicated on some occasions by the external influence of government economic policy.

When the scales of power go out of equilibrium and tip, the effect can easily lead to dispute. History tells us that the collective will of workers will unite, combine and fight back to protect their pay and employment conditions and we do not have to look back too far to see the impact this has had on employers, on workers and indeed on governments.

Take some time to think of where would you place your own organisation in terms of the scales of power e.g.is it equilibrium? Or is it tipped in favour of the Business? Or the employees? Do you think this is the best balance for sustained business success?

Where I would place my business on the Scales of Power (tick the appropriate box)					
In Equilibrium		In Favour of the Business		In Favour of the Employees	

What could you change to provide a better balance? List your ideas below:

Actions to improve the balance of power
1..
2.
3.
4.
5.

If management and trade union relationships are not well developed e.g. working at stage three of the MAP, disputes can easily take hold and escalate. When this happens, it becomes even more difficult to achieve the recipe for success and rebalance the scales of power.

The Rabble Rousers

The reality is many managers have a negative perception of trade unions and these views have often been informed by the high-profile strikes and industrial disputes, particularly during the 1970s and 1980s. These disputes have left a long and dark shadow, and a brief look back at some events will help develop a foundation of knowledge which will benefit you as you work through the MAP and help you develop your tailored route to success within your own organisation.

In the 1970s and 1980s it was commonplace to see animated, rabble rousing union officials on national television leading picket lines or convening union meetings in the car parks of some of the UK's largest engineering and manufacturing plants up and down the country. Often, at the heart of these disputes were demands for higher and higher pay increases and increasing concerns over (and resistance to) the emergence of new technologies. Unemployment was rising, inflation had spiralled to 28% and average wage rises were averaging 26% (Source: National Archives).

In 1970 there were around 5,000 strikes resulting in over 27 million lost working days and many argue such action played a large part in the demise of the UK as a dominant force in the motor vehicle manufacturing and other heavy engineering industries. It should be stressed that all the blame for this cannot lie solely at the door of the trade unions; there were complex economic circumstances and the reality was that many of the management practices of the day were not above reproach.

The Political Factor

Then of course there was the political factor and it is widely reported that the miners strikes of 1972 and 1974 played a significant part in the fall of the Conservative government of the day (under the Premiership of Edward Heath). By the mid-1970s even the Labour party was becoming increasingly concerned by the actions of the trade unions, prompting amongst other things the then Labour Prime Minister Harold Wilson to separate the Conciliation and Advisory Service from government, and rename this the Conciliation and Arbitration Service. He then expanded the service and renamed it the Advisory, Conciliation and Arbitration Service (ACAS) with an increased focus on helping resolve work place disputes. The Employment Act 1975 made ACAS a statutory body and in its first year it helped resolve 2,500 disputes.

Callaghan took over as Labour leader and Prime Minister following the resignation of Harold Wilson in 1976. By this time, the government was in serious financial trouble and had to cut back on spending, which brought it into conflict with the trade unions and in 1978/1979 Callaghan faced widespread industrial disputes across the country, including strikes from teachers, health workers and local government employees and the prospect of a new pay demand from the miners. This was commonly referred to as the 'Winter of Discontent' and forced Callaghan to call another election which Labour lost.

Much of the electorate were becoming disillusioned with Labour's policies on trade unions and wanted a government that would control the extremists. The Conservatives had a new leader who promised to do exactly that – her name was Margaret Thatcher and in 1979 she became Prime Minister. This would prove to be a watershed moment in post war industrial / trade union relations and her sights were firmly set on the National Union of Mineworkers.

The Miners' Strike

Many people still have vivid memories of the high-profile and highly emotive miners' strike in 1984-85. Some say this was the bitterest industrial dispute in British history, which at its peak involved over 145,000 mineworkers. It was a highly political and emotive dispute, with the National Union of Mineworkers (NUM) taking strike action to shut down the coal industry in a move designed to apply pressure to the government to prevent wage restraint and colliery closures. Earlier, the 1972 and 1974 strikes by the NUM had played a significant role in bringing down the Conservative government and similarly they played a significant role in the 'Winter of Discontent' and the subsequent fall of the Labour government.

Many independent bystanders saw the 1984/85 miner's strike as a 'winner takes all' contest between the leader of the NUM, Arthur Scargill and the then Prime Minister, Margaret Thatcher. It was widely reported in the media that Thatcher referred to Scargill as 'the enemy within' and had formed the view she must do everything in her power to defeat Scargill. In September 1984 the strike was ruled illegal, as no national ballot had been held, and soon after the 51-week long strike was over. Following this, deep coal mining in Great Britain would never be the same again. From a base of 174 mines in 1983, a much-reduced coal industry was privatised in 1994 and following further decline, the last deep mine in Great Britain closed in December 2015. Coal mines, and along with it the National Union of Mineworkers, were consigned to the history books.

New Technology – Old Issues

In 1986 there was another long-running and bloody strike, this time by the print workers trade union, the National Graphical Association (NGA). The dispute came to a head in 1986 when the Murdoch Group moved newspaper production from Fleet Street (the historic heart of newspaper production) to

Wapping in outer London. More significantly the new production process would use computers to allow journalists to directly input copy, rather than involve print workers who were insisting on using outdated 'hot-metal' linotype printing methods. One could argue these printers and the NGA were modern-day Luddites resisting the introduction of new technology and thwarting the industry's ability to adapt and change, despite an offer by the company of some significant redundancy payments.

Some argue the trade union was simply trying to protect jobs and security of income for their members. The Wapping dispute, like the miners' strike a year before, was high-profile and marred by bloody conflict on the picket lines. Hundreds of Police officers were injured, and 1,500 pickets were arrested. The strike ran for longer than the earlier miner's strike - 54 weeks in total, albeit with 6,000 strikers as opposed to 145,000 striking miners. But, as with the miners before, the strike came to a devastating conclusion for the striking printers. All striking printers were dismissed and what was to follow was a widespread adoption of modern newspaper publishing practices across the whole print industry. Print production of newspapers would never be the same again.

Brothers and Sisters Dis-united

Of particular note, and very different from the miner's situation, was the role other unions played in the dispute, not as 'brothers and sisters in arms', rather as opportunists who seized the moment, who were willing to embrace the new working practices and collaborate with the Murdoch Group to set up and operate the new plant. In return they would secure a single union recognition agreement. The result of these new working practices meant the same number of newspapers were produced with 670 workers whereas previously it took 6,800!

The miners' and the printers' strikes of the mid 1980s were defining moments in the history of trade unions. It can be argued these, and other industrial disputes of the time, were a trigger for a series of changes to trade union and employment legislation and with them a corresponding significant drop in trade union membership. The impact on reduced strike action was dramatic and the number of days lost due to industrial action dropped from 27 million lost days of work in 1979, due to industrial disputes, to a record low of 170,000 days in 2016.

2010 to the Present Day

Whilst their membership levels may have significantly declined, trade unions still have a considerable presence and although the number of days lost due to industrial action has significantly reduced, strikes and other forms of action are by no means a thing of the past. There have been several significant industrial disputes that act as a reminder of the ability of workers to unite, combine and take action when they believe there has been an unfair tip in the balance of power and their conditions of employment are under threat.

In 2011 there was a national public-sector worker strike in protest against pension reforms. This strike involved over 2 million public-sector workers, the highest number of workers ever involved in strike action. I was a Director of HR in the public sector at this time and recall the general mood was very different to other disputes and strikes I have managed. The protest was very much against government (quite a common issue in the many high-profile strikes) and on this occasion, there was little internal dispute between workers and their respective employers. Maybe this was because all public-sector workers, from the Chief Executive down, would be affected by the reforms, irrespective of whether they were a member of a trade union or not.

The trade unions tended to be very mindful to work with management to ensure critical public services were maintained and willing to agree exemption for certain workers to remain at work. Furthermore, it was only a one day stoppage, hence it was more a demonstration against government and a show of collective strength as opposed to the typical industrial disputes of the 1970s and 1980s. This helped the trade unions maintain a degree of public support and enabled working relationships with their employers to be maintained, hence avoiding the damaging legacy often left in the aftermath of strike action.

Despite the rhetoric of the government, the collective voice of 2 million workers could not be ignored and the trade unions achieved significant concessions to the proposed reforms.

Proposed changes to pension schemes have triggered a similar reaction amongst staff in the private sector, e.g. in 2011 2,500 employees at Unilever, a major household name and FTSE top 100 company, commenced an 11-day period of strike action across 12 sites throughout the UK. This was the first strike in their history.

In 2016 proposed changes to the terms and conditions triggered strike action from junior doctors in the NHS. This was another historic first and signalled an unprecedented shift in willingness to take strike action to defend working conditions and resist what was considered unfair reform. Interestingly, there was a high degree of public support for the junior doctors and this might be reflective of a shift in the mood of workers generally to challenge more vigorously and to defend their terms and conditions.

A feature of the current employment landscape is the growing GIG economy and use of zero hours contracts. Proponents argue this offers workers flexibility and choice, whereas others see it as modern-day exploitation from the rich and powerful. However, there have been several recent high-profile media campaigns and trade union-backed industrial action in relation to zero-hour contracts and minimum wage compliance. This, together with some landmark court rulings, e.g. Pimlico Plumbers and Uber cases, in relation to employment status and entitlement to certain employment benefits, shows that when the scales of power tip, worker representation and public support can galvanise in order to redress the balance and protect and fairly reward workers. The GIG economy is a rich seam of potential membership for trade unions and this is now being actively targeted by the TUC.

Trade unions still have a significant presence across the employment landscape and there is potential for this membership to once again grow. Likewise, the potential for employee relations to break down, for the balance of power to tip and for disputes to escalate, is still very real.

Understandably strike action grabs the headlines, but businesses need to be aware that action short of strike can be just as debilitating for the business e.g. work to rule, overtime bans, etc. Such action can quickly lead to drop in staff morale, increased sickness absence, high staff turnover, drop in production, increased errors, drop in quality, etc. and this type of industrial action can be difficult to resolve. The consequences can impact massively on the bottom line e.g. lost profit, poor service, loss of customer confidence and long-term reputational damage.

A core strength of trade unions is their ability to organise themselves and galvanise the collective strength of their members to protect or improve their employment terms and conditions. However, trade unions have a responsibility to achieve this in a way that also protects the long-term job security of their members. This means trade unions should also work with employers to adapt to changing business demands and to help them grow and prosper. As Charles Darwin identified, 'it is not the strongest that survive, but those most adaptable to change'. History tells us that as one company or industry flounders, another emerges, and likewise as one union fails to embrace changes, there may well be another who will. The one constant for businesses and trade unions is change.

Friend or Foe?

There is a risk that in briefly looking back over the history of trade unions you are left with a picture of bloody conflict and negativity. However, without the significant influence of trade unions and their collective bargaining and without significant sacrifice and pain incurred by many trade union members over the decades fighting for improved terms and conditions, many of us would not be enjoying benefits today that are generally taken for granted.

Maybe the question for companies is not 'what have trade unions done for us?' but rather 'what could they do for us?' There is undisputable evidence that an engaged workforce is a more effective and productive workforce. Trade unions, and how effectively you work with them, can have a significant influence on the levels of engagement between employers and their employees, and we will look at this in further detail in chapter 4.

It can be strongly argued that recognition of mutual advantage identified one hundred and fifty years ago is as relevant today as it was then and remains at the core of effective working relationships with trade unions.

Chapter Summary

The diagram below summarises how over the last two hundred years trade unions have triumphed, despite sustained efforts to supress them. We have highlighted their resolve to fight for fair working conditions and seen their place in the industrial landscape become an accepted norm. We have charted their rise to a peak during the 1970s and 1980s to a rapid decline, in large part due to the Thatcher reforms. However, membership levels have stabilised and trade unions remain a considerable influence.

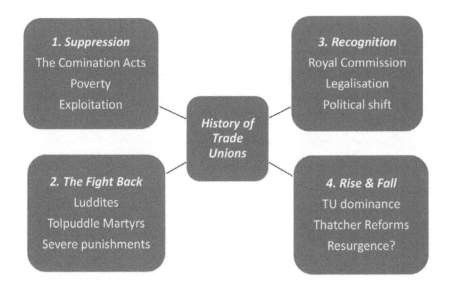

Key Points

1. Trade unions have been around for over two hundred years.
2. Membership levels are now broadly stable at 6.6 million members.
3. Strike action is the action of last resort to enable workers to redress the balance of power.
4. Trade unions have played a massive role in improving working terms and conditions of workers across all sectors and all industries.
5. There is little doubt that strikes are high risk and it is in everyone's best interest to reach a negotiated settlement before this point is reached.
6. Change can be worrying for trade union members and this can manifest in resistance and ultimately conflict.

7. The evidence for partnership working is compelling. Trade unions can bring considerable skill, knowledge and experience to the table and they are well attuned to the needs and aspirations of their members.
8. Together everyone can prosper.

Chapter 3:
Trade Unions and the Law

Introduction

Whilst the law gives trade unions certain statutory rights, by and large much of the employment law since the 1980s has sought to limit the power of trade unions. In general, the law has been systematically changed to mainly constrain the ability of trade unions to influence strike action and thwart the use of extreme tactics by some trade union members to influence or coerce others into voting for industrial disputes, some of which could be argued was simply bullying and intimidation.

I recall quite vividly, in my early career in engineering, attending union meetings in the car park and witnessing first-hand the intimidation tactics to 'encourage' the appropriate response to the call of the shop steward: 'all those in favour' i.e. in favour of strike action. Those in favour of the proposed action left others in no doubt as to how they felt they should be voting. Clearly many people were coerced into voting for strike action when they really didn't want to.

The legislative reforms have banished such practices, and few would argue for their return. Margaret Thatcher's Conservative governments in the 1980s and 1990 instigated most of these changes, and notably the

Working Positively with Trade Unions

Labour party on their return to power in 1997, under the leadership of Tony Blair, did little to repeal the 'Thatcher' reforms. The reality was the public were fed up with strikes and did not want to see a return to the 1970s/80s industrial trouble and strife.

The aim of this chapter is to provide an overview of the key elements of employment law that will enhance your knowledge and provide a sound basis on which to help build effective working relationships with trade unions. We will cover the legislative framework in relation to trade union recognition and de-recognition; who can join a trade union; strike action; individual rights; and the rights of shop stewards. Most of the legislation in relation to trade unions has been consolidated in the Trade Union and Labour Relations Act 1992. This is a hefty document of more than 200 pages and can be accessed at www.legislation.gov.uk

Let us now look at how much you know about the legislation regarding trade unions. Have a go at the short quiz below to test your knowledge. Be as honest as you can and be prepared to say that you don't know.

QUIZ

Q1. Can any employee join a trade union?
Q2. Can an employee be a member of more than one trade union?
Q3. Which main piece of legislation covers trade union membership?
Q4. Do I have to recognise a trade union?
Q5. Can I de-recognise a trade union?
Q6. What is a closed shop?
Q7. What is the benefit of recognising a trade union?

Working Positively with Trade Unions

> Q8. If a trade union requests recognition can I refuse?
> Q9. Do I have to give a shop steward paid time off for union duties?
> Q10. Which sector has the most strikes: public or private?

I hope you found that useful. It will help you identify any gaps in your knowledge. We will try to fill in as many of those gaps as possible as we progress through the rest of this chapter.

Trade Union Recognition

First let's start with trade union recognition and what this means. An employer recognises a trade union when they either voluntarily agree, or are statutorily compelled, to collectively negotiate with a trade union (or unions) on behalf of a designated group of employees (often referred to as a bargaining unit) on matters of terms and conditions of employment, for example pay, hours of work and holidays. The things they will collectively bargain i.e. negotiate on are normally be formalised in a written collective agreement.

Employers that do not currently recognise a trade union could receive a request for recognition at any time if the union has at least 10% union membership within the proposed bargaining unit and they have evidence that a majority of employees are in favour of recognition. If a request is made, then this must be in writing and the trade union must ask the employer to voluntarily recognise them.

The Role of the Central Arbitration Committee (CAC)

The employer must reply within 10 working days and either accept or reject the request. If the employer accepts this request, then within 20 days (or longer by agreement) they need to agree the bargaining unit (who will be covered by the agreement). If the request is refused, and the employer has more than 21 employees, the trade union can make a formal request for recognition to the Central Arbitration Committee (CAC). Requests to the CAC must be:

- in writing
- state the name of union
- specify which group(s) of employees will be represented i.e. the proposed bargaining unit
- state that the union is making the request under Schedule A1 of the Trade Union and Labour Relations (Consolidation) Act 1992

Be Aware

Employers need to be aware that unless they challenge the application, the CAC will accept the trade union's application for recognition if it meets certain requirements i.e. if they have at least 10% union membership within the proposed bargaining unit and they have evidence that a majority of employees are in favour of recognition.

A trade union has no statutory right to make a formal request for recognition if:

- they have applied for recognition in the last 3 years
- they are not a certified independent union
- there's already a recognition agreement that allows another union to represent employees in the bargaining unit
- another union - representing 10% of the employees in the proposed bargaining unit - has already applied to CAC

The Bargaining Unit

When the CAC accepts a trade union's application the employer needs to start discussions about which employees the union will represent. When this cannot be agreed between the employer and the unit, the CAC will decide, and the employer is obliged to provide the CAC with specific information such as:

- a list of the categories of employees who will be in the proposed bargaining unit, e.g. technical and skilled, but not managers
- a list of the places where they work
- the number of employees in each category at each workplace

In forming their decision, the CAC will normally hold a hearing and decide the bargaining unit based on a number of things, including the views of the employer and those of the union and what other bargaining arrangements already exist. When the bargaining unit is decided the CAC may appoint a 'suitable independent person' (SIP) to communicate with employees in the bargaining unit. If this happens, the employer has to give the SIP the names and addresses of employees in the proposed bargaining unit and if this is not provided the employer will get a 'remedial order' from CAC. The order must be complied with or the CAC could declare that the employer must recognise the union.

Subject to Ballot

However, agreeing the bargaining unit does not, in itself, mean you must recognise the trade union. This may be subject to a ballot, in particular if less than 50% of the employees in the bargaining unit are not members of the trade union. The CAC will decide if there needs to be a ballot of employees in the bargaining unit (both union members and non-union members) and the CAC will conduct this ballot.

The CAC has detailed procedures to inform this, including making sure the employer allows the union access to talk to employees in the bargaining unit without management being present. The employer cannot threaten or take any action against a worker because they attended a meeting and the union can complain to CAC if they think the employer has not co-operated.

The result of the vote will be announced 48 hours after the ballot closes and the CAC will declare the trade union is recognised if both:
- the majority of employees in the ballot vote to recognise the union
- at least 40% of the employees in the bargaining unit vote to recognise the union

If CAC declares the trade union is recognised the employer must work with the union and work out how to collectively bargain on matters of pay, hours and holiday entitlements. If CAC declares the trade union is not recognised, the union will not be able to apply for statutory recognition for 3 years, but employers could still recognise them voluntarily, which would be unlikely if the request had been refused in the first instance.

Detailed guidance on trade union recognition is available at: https://www.gov.uk/trade-union-recognition-employers/statutory-recognition

Let us take a look at your organisation and list below the unions that are recognised and the areas of the organisation they cover. If you do not recognise a trade union, identify which union could potentially represent different groups. This will help you identify where you might get a claim for recognition in the future.

Which trade unions do you recognise?	Areas of the business covered
1. 2. 3.	1. 2. 3.

Which trade might approach you for recognition rights?	For which areas of the business?
1. 2. 3.	1. 2. 3.

I hope you found that useful. If you could not identify specific areas of recognition it may indicate that your agreement is vague. If that is the case it would be worth reviewing your agreement(s).

What About De-recognising a Trade Union?

An employer cannot simply de-recognise a trade union just because it wants to. That might sound like a statement of the obvious, but some employers think they can do this. However, if the workers in the agreed bargaining unit no longer support the recognition agreement and don't want the trade union (which they may or may not be a member of) to negotiate on their behalf, you can seek to de-recognise the trade union. This is unusual, but if this does materialise there are two options, voluntary de-recognition or formal de-recognition through the CAC.

It is unlikely a trade union will give up their hard-earned recognition rights and therefore you would need to go through the CAC and follow a similar process to that for recognition.

Who Can Join a Trade Union?

Anyone can apply to join a trade union, or indeed be a member of more than one union, and acceptance of membership is solely a matter for the trade union(s) to whom an individual has applied to join, and it has nothing to do with the employer.

A trade union may advertise and campaign for members but cannot intimidate or coerce employees to join a trade union. Any advertising or campaigning in the workplace can only be done with the employer's permission, and the employer can refuse this.

Closure of the Closed Shop

Even if the employer recognises a trade union(s) for collective bargaining purposes, it is still a matter of choice for each individual employee whether to join that (or any other) trade union. Long gone are the days of the 'closed shop', a term that describes a workplace where the employer has agreed with the trade union that all employees must be a member of the union, and previously this would have formed a condition of their employment requiring them to remain a member of the union throughout their employment with that employer.

> I had first-hand experience of this and I recall vividly my first day at work in 1977 when the person who met and welcomed me was not the works manager, rather the shop steward who presented me with a form to sign. When I queried what the form was I was told it was my membership form to join the National Union of Railwaymen (NUR). When I further queried why the NUR (my employment had nothing to do with railways), he explained if I wanted to start work here I had no choice but to sign as the NUR were the recognised union and had a closed shop agreement with the employer. As a young 16-year-old fresh out of school I found this very strange but signed and got on with it. I should point out that this was a positive experience and indeed I went on to be elected as shop steward just two years later at the age of eighteen.

Closed shops were commonplace in the 1970s and typified the strength that trade unions had cemented across great swathes of British industry at that time.

One of Thatcher's early trade union reforms following her election as Prime Minister in 1979 was the Employment Act 1980, which amongst many others thing required an 80% ballot needed to legalise a closed shop. This, together with a requirement under the Employment Act 1982 that extended the 80% rule on closed shops to every 5 years, pretty much brought an end to this practice.

Free Riders

Many people attribute this to the start of the major decline in trade union membership that followed. However, there are still many examples of where trade unions are recognised, but not all employees are members of the recognised unions. The crucial point is that this is an individual choice and it is not necessarily a negative reflection on trade unions. I recall in one of my most recent employments with a major public-sector organisation, where collective bargaining was well established and there was excellent partnership working with the recognised trade unions, only 40% of the employees were a member of a trade union. But the unions negotiated on behalf of everyone in the bargaining unit (which covered the whole workforce in this example) and thus the other 60% of non-union employees benefited from the collective agreements.

This is not an unusual situation and can lead to some people arguing the non-union employees are 'free-riding' on the back of the fee-paying union members. Employers need to be aware of this scenario as there is potential for it to create divisions in the workplace, particularly at times of pay negotiations, etc.

A further important point for employers to be aware of is whilst they may be negotiating with a trade union on behalf of the bargaining unit, the trade union are only obliged to consult and communicate with their members and not necessarily all employees in the bargaining unit i.e. the non-union members. Equally, if there is a failure to agree and the union instigate a ballot for industrial action, they will only ballot their members within the bargaining unit.

There is a risk in these circumstances that some trade union members could apply pressure on non-union colleagues to join and make derogatory comments in relation to them not being in the trade union but receiving the benefits of the union bargaining on their behalf. Such behaviour would very likely constitute bullying and harassment and should not be tolerated and should be addressed swiftly if it is ever identified.

Division of Labour

Of course, it can be of benefit to the employer, even where they recognise a trade union for the purposes of collective bargaining, not to have all their employees in the union. This can provide the employer with a degree of useful division of labour if an industrial dispute situation occurs, as the non-union employees (1) would be unlikely to participate in the dispute and (2) if they did they would not have the statutory protection afforded to union members (assuming the trade union conducts a proper ballot for industrial action). However, it must be stressed that it is illegal for employers to offer an incentive to an employee to either join, not to join or to leave a trade union.

Individual Right to join a Trade Union

Of course, many employers do not recognise a trade union, but this does not change an employee's right to still join a trade union. A common question is why would they when their union cannot negotiate changes/

improvements to their terms and conditions? The answer is mainly to secure representation in disciplinary and grievance situations, in case of unfair or wrongful dismissal, or to assist them to bring a case against their employer through the Employment Tribunal, for example if they feel they have been discriminated against.

I have come across many cases where an employee has tried to join a trade union at a point where they have become subject to a disciplinary procedure, which is like trying to join the RAC at the point your car breaks down. Any application to join a trade union is a matter for the trade union in question, but they will generally have rules to cover such situations and they may have qualifying criteria that prevent this type of situation.

Dealing with Industrial Action

We can see from the brief recap of recent history in chapter 2 the potentially catastrophic impact industrial disputes, most notably strike action, can have on business, communities and indeed the nation. Anyone who has been in the situation of having to manage an industrial strike will tell you that these can end up complex, sensitive and difficult situations to resolve and, like any breakdown in a relationship, it is far more difficult to recover once the relationship has broken down than it is to resolve the situation at an earlier stage.

The statistics tell us strikes are far less prevalent today than they were in the 1970s and 1980s, but they are still a very real possibility. The reality is that many strikes are threatened and never materialise, this threat is a key component of the trade union negotiating tool kit. There is a well coined phrase used by shop stewards 'we reserve the right to withdraw our labour'. This is true, but it is subject to quite stringent legislation and procedural compliance.

Having a good understanding of these requirements will give HR practitioners and managers greater confidence to handle such threats (which is sometimes nothing more than aggressive negotiating tactics). However, it can be a high stakes game of 'call my bluff' and a sound working understanding of the relevant legislation can be of immense help to HR practitioners and managers who are dealing with such situations. For example, even if the trade union threaten industrial action there is a detailed process they must follow to ensure legal compliance, and this can take several weeks. Failure to follow makes them vulnerable to being sued. We will cover this in more detail below.

In this chapter, we will summarise the legislative changes that have transformed the process of organising and executing strike action and will provide an overview of the main recent legislative requirements that must be complied with by trade unions should they pursue strike action (or action short of a strike) and if such a strike materialises, what the union can and cannot do.

When looking at the history of trade unions in the previous chapter it can be seen how successive governments have put in place, modified or maintained legislation that regulates and controls the rights of trade unions to invoke industrial action, and especially strike action.

Ballots, Strikes and Pickets

Looking back, even over a relatively short time of the last 30 years or so, it is quite incredible to think that there was no need for a ballot or any need to serve notice of intention to go on strike or give any detail of who was going to go on strike. Unions had absolute protection in law and secondary action was also lawful, meaning a trade union from a completely different organisation could also come out on strike in support of the dispute that had nothing to do with them. Striking workers could amass at the gates of the employer with whom there was a dispute and picket i.e. protest and thwart the ability of the company to function.

Thatcher made it her business to change this and started her process of incremental reform with the Employment Acts 1980 and 1982. These Acts made trade unions liable for their action, restricted lawful picketing, created restrictions on secondary action and narrowed the definition of a trade dispute. The Trade Union Act 1984 came next and introduced secret ballots when electing union officials and as a precondition before industrial action. The Public Order Act 1986 followed, and this required written notice of public assembly and the Employment Act 1990 abolished secondary action.

There was then a period of about 8 years or so before the next set of reforms, which came in the guise of the Employment Acts 1988 and 1990. These Acts went a step further and made trade unions liable to compensate members whom they had disciplined (within the context of their Rule Book) for non-compliance of majority decisions, gave individual members the ability to seek an injunction to the proposed action if no pre-strike ballot had been undertaken and set a requirement for ballots for separate workplaces.

The final piece of the 'Thatcher' reforms came in the form of the Trade Union Reform and Employment Rights Act 1993 which introduced the requirement for all industrial action ballots to be postal. These reforms became consolidated within the Trade Union and Labour Relations Act 1992, and this remains a pivotal piece of employment legislation which brings together all collective employment rights, including trade union finances and elections, union member rights, including dismissal, time off, redundancy consultation and industrial action legislation. It defines trade unions, their legal rights and duties, and protects the right of workers to join or leave a union without suffering discrimination or detriment.

However, whilst the reforms have undeniably had the impact of curtailing strike action, they have by no means eradicated them, and they never will.

Political parties of all persuasions respect the basic premise that the 'right to strike' is a fundamental element of collective bargaining, and ultimately is the only way workers (who are trade union members) can exercise some balance of power against employers who, in their view, are not prepared to pay decent wages and provide fair working conditions. Employers must remain vigilant to the potential for industrial dispute. In 2016 there were 488 industrial action ballots, 466 of which called for strike action and 436 (94%) resulted in a majority vote for action.

This tells us if an employer gets to a position where a vote for action has been called, it is highly likely members will vote in favour. What is particularly noteworthy is the 436 positive ballots for strike resulted in only 101 stoppages (23%) and the majority of strikes (60%) were in the private sector. This is the highest level of stoppages in the private sector since 2005 (Source: Labour Disputes in the UK 2016, Office of National Statistics). In 2016 there was a total of 322,000 working days lost due to industrial action, mainly due to large-scale public-sector strikes such as the junior doctors' strike.

Main Source of Dispute

Pay remains the principle reason for strike action. Interestingly the private sector has had more strikes than the public sector in the last three years, and whilst the public sector has lost the most working days, the private sector still lost 79,000 working days as a result of 60 stoppages. The impact on production, productivity, reputational damage, and the time and effort needed to resolve the issues post-strike should not be underestimated. We know strike action can leave a dark shadow and even when the strike is ended, the negative impact on employee relations can continue for a long time.

Trade Union Act 2016

The impact of strikes, particularly public-sector strikes, can extend far beyond the direct impact on the employer. Stoppages of public services such as education, transport and health can affect tens of thousands of members of the public going about their everyday life, and this was reflected in the Briefing Paper on the Trade Union Bill (CBP 7295, 7 September 2015). The paper highlights one of the main purposes of the Bill (now enacted as the Trade Union Act 2016) which was to 'Ensure hardworking people are not disrupted by little supported strike action'.

For example, the impact of the teachers' strike in 2011, which saw closures across two thirds of our schools, was estimated to have caused a £480m decrease in output across UK industries. Many people were directly or indirectly affected e.g. parents having to arrange childcare or employers having to deal with parents, family or friends having to take time off at short notice to look after children unable to attend school, etc.

Similarly, thousands of patients and their families were adversely affected by the high-profile junior doctors' strikes in 2016 which resulted in 129,000 working days being lost and consequently patients faced delays of weeks and months for planned procedures, bringing about massive frustration, inconvenience and in some cases direct negative impact on their health. However, the strikers achieved significant concessions they would otherwise not have got and therefore will feel their actions were necessary and vindicated. It is a powerful example of the strength of trade unions to galvanise the masses.

The Trade Union Bill subsequently went through parliament, received Royal Assent and was placed on the statute as the Trade Union Act 2016. Amongst other things it introduced even more stringent industrial ballot conditions, most notably:

- The requirement for an increased 50% voting threshold, whilst maintaining the requirement for majority vote in favour of action.
- An additional requirement that 40% of all those entitled in the ballot

must vote in favour of action in certain public services e.g. transport, education, fire and health.
- Requires more detail of the trade dispute on the ballot paper. Previously there was only a requirement to give two choices: Strike Action or Action short of Strike. Now they must detail what action short of strike means; when action will start and how long action will last, and a summary of the terms negotiated for.
- Increased notice of strike action from 7 to 14 days.
- Introduced time limits on the mandate to take action.

We can see from the statistics above that whilst 94% of ballots receive a majority vote for strike action, only 23% result in actual strike action. This begs the question why is it not possible to negotiate an acceptable settlement before getting to that stage, by which point negotiations are likely to have been long and protracted.

In these circumstances, the outcome is either management backing down and conceding to the demands of the union, or the union backing down and accepting a lesser deal than they had desired (which would be unlikely, having gone through a strike ballot and got a majority mandate). The result, whatever way you look at this, is a Win-Lose situation which is not conducive to good employee relations and securing business success. We will cover this in more detail later in the next chapter where we will introduce you to the MAP to Positive Working Relationships with Trade Unions.

A Summary of the Reforms

Since 1979 there have been 12 major legislative changes to the legislative landscape affecting trade unions. These Acts of Parliament are summarised below as a quick reference guide. What is particularly notable is that of the 12 Acts, 9 were associated with the Thatcher reforms from 1979 to 1993 and, despite their return to power in 1997, Labour did little to change the Thatcher reforms during their decade-long period of government.

Reform	Government	Changes in Relation to Industrial Action
Employment Act 1980	Conservative	• Restricted lawful picketing to own place of work • Restricted right to take secondary action • Code of practice (six pickets)
Employment Act 1982	Conservative	• Further restrictions on industrial action – narrowed the definition of trade dispute • Restricted action to own employer • Introduced injunctions against unions and to sue for damages
Trade Union Act 1984	Conservative	• Introduced requirement for secret ballots for the election of trade union officials and industrial action
Public Order Act 1986	Conservative	• New criminal offences in relation to picketing
Employment Act 1988	Conservative	• Unions to compensate members disciplined for non-compliance with majority decisions • Members can seek injunctions if no pre-strike ballot • Union finances to be open to inspection • Unions prevented from paying members' or officials' fines • Action to preserve post-entry closed shop made unlawful • New restrictions on industrial action and election ballots • Ballots for separate workplaces

Working Positively with Trade Unions

Employment Act 1990	Conservative	• All secondary action unlawful • Union liable for action induced by any union official unless written repudiation using a statutory form of words sent to all members • Selective dismissal of strikers taking unofficial action
Trade Union and Labour Relations Act 1992	Conservative	• The Act defines the meaning of 'trade union' and sets out the: • Rights of trade unions members • Rights not to be refused employment on grounds of being, or not, a trade union member • Rights in relation to trade union recognition and collective bargaining • Time off for trade union duties and activities • Rules in relation to industrial actions • The function of ACAS
Trade Union Reform and Employment Rights Act 1993	Conservative	• Independent scrutiny of strike ballots • All industrial action ballots to be postal
Employment Relations Act 1999	Labour	• Dismissal for participation in official industrial action deemed unfair within a protected period of 8 weeks • Ballot and notice provisions for strike or industrial action

Act	Party	Provisions
Employee Relations Act, 2004	Labour	• Provisions to increase the protections against the dismissal of employees taking official, lawfully-organised industrial action by extending the "protected period" from 8 to 12 weeks; exempting "lock out" days from the 12-week protected period • Procedural steps to resolve industrial disputes and measures to simplify the law on industrial action ballots and ballot notices • Industrial action ballots • Built on earlier White Paper: Fairness at Work (1998) • Move away from conflict to partnership • Balance of rights and responsibilities • Importance of ACAS
Trade Union Act 2016	Conservative	• Funds to be provided to assist in developing employment partnerships • More stringent ballot rules • Increased 50% voting threshold and maintains the requirement for a majority vote in favour of action • Introduced a further threshold i.e. that an additional 40% of all those entitled in the ballot must vote in favour of action in certain public services e.g. transport, education, fire and health • Requires more detail of the trade dispute on the ballot paper. Previously there was only a requirement to give two choices: Strike Action or Action short of Strike. Now they must detail what 'Action short of Strike' means, when action will start and how long action will last, and a summary of the terms negotiated for • Union required to appoint a picket supervisor • Increased notice of strike action from 7 to 14 days • Introduced time limits on the mandate to take industrial action • Requirement for a positive opt-in to the political fund

The Law and Shop Stewards

We have already identified that work place representatives, often termed shop stewards, are key individuals in the union/management relationship. In organisations that recognise a trade union, the role of shop steward is to support and represent the views of their members, both individually and collectively. Their role as workplace representative will typically include getting involved in negotiations on pay and other terms and conditions, representation at discipline and grievance meetings, dealing with health, safety and learning concerns, dealing with issues in relation to grading e.g. job evaluation, and equal pay.

They may also have a wider union remit to recruit and organise members, to promote the union and to get involved in union campaigns, both regionally and nationally. Depending on the size of the union membership, trade unions sometimes have different representative (rep) roles e.g. Health & Safety rep, Equality & Diversity rep, Union Learning rep. However, it is important to remember shop stewards are first and foremost employees and must fulfil their contract of employment the same as any other employee.

Workplace representatives are elected in accordance with the trade union rules and, once elected, the trade union will arrange for necessary shop steward training and will notify the employer (in cases where the employer recognises the trade union) and provide the details of the person who has been elected to act as an accredited representative of the union. If this is not received, the employer has the right to ask the union for this confirmation.

Trade Union Facilities

Once an employee is elected as a workplace union representative, and accredited by their trade union, they are entitled (under section 168 of the Trade Union and Labour Relations Act 1992) (TULRA) to reasonable time off in work hours to carry out certain trade union duties and activities. The ACAS Code of Practice 3: 'Time off for trade union duties and activities', provides detailed guidance on the time off (paid and unpaid) that representatives are entitled to. The precise detail of what they are entitled to will vary from organisation to organisation and will be informed by the trade union recognition agreement and machinery of negotiation agreed with the union as part of that recognition.

TULRA requires ACAS to provide practical guidance on the time off to be permitted by an employer and they have a freely available code on *Time Off for Trade Union Duties and Activities* (available at http://www.acas.org.uk). The code includes time off for Union Learning Representatives (ULRs).

There are separate regulations, The Safety Representatives and Safety Committees Regulations 1977, regulation 4(2)(a), covering union Health and Safety representatives and these require that employers allow union Health and Safety representatives paid time, as is necessary, during working hours, to perform their functions.

ACAS state the general purpose of the statutory provisions and this Code of Practice is to aid and improve the effectiveness of relationships between employers and trade unions. Employers and unions have a joint responsibility to ensure that agreed arrangements work to mutual advantage by specifying how reasonable time off for union duties and activities and for training will work.

Trade Union Duties and Activities Include:
- Negotiations on terms and conditions e.g. pay, pensions, sick pay arrangements, holiday entitlements.
- Equality & Diversity.
- Engagement or non-engagement, or termination or suspension of

employment e.g. recruitment and selection policies, redundancy and dismissal, etc.
- Allocation of work or the duties of employment as between workers or groups of workers e.g. job grading, job evaluation, flexible working, etc.
- Matters of discipline e.g. disciplinary procedures, representing or accompanying employees at internal interviews, appearing at an Employment Tribunal.
- Trade union membership or non-membership e.g. representational arrangements, any union involvement in the induction of new workers.

You must also provide reasonable facilities to the trade union representatives e.g. accommodation and equipment.

In organisations that do not recognise a trade union, the union representative will have a more limited role focused more on individual support and representation e.g. the Employee Relations Act 1999 gives every worker a right to be accompanied at disciplinary and grievance hearings by a fellow worker or 'companion'. Shop stewards can fulfil this role for their members whether the union is recognised or not. However, they will not be entitled to paid time off for other duties and activities afforded to elected representatives where the union is recognised. That said, the employer should consider reasonable requests for unpaid leave.

Let us now just look at any areas you feel you need to know more about.

List below any concerns or questions you may have about trade unions and the law
1.
2.
3.
4.
5.
6.
7.
8.
9.
10.

You now need to get the answers to these questions so that you can deal effectively in these areas, if questioned in the future. There are many sources to help you get answers if these are not sufficiently covered in the book e.g. you may have access to an employment lawyer or an HR specialist. If not, there are some excellent resources available on-line, and there are numerous services you can subscribe to. ACAS provide some excellent guides and have a very useful helpline facility. The Chartered Institute of Personnel and Development (CIPD) is a rich source and members have access to a wide range of services, fact sheets and other information. Use these to get your answers and further enhance your knowledge.

Working Positively with Trade Unions

Key Points

1. Anyone can join a trade union, whether the union is recognised or not.

2. A trade union can seek to be recognised, providing certain conditions are met.

3. The Thatcher reforms significantly curbed the power of the trade unions.

4. Threat of strike action is still very real (628 strike ballots in 2016).

5. There are stringent rules on strike ballots that trade unions MUST comply with.

6. Much of the law in relation to trade union rights is contained in the Trade Union and Labour Relations (consolidated) Act, 1992.

7. There ae approximately 6.6 million trade union members in employment in the UK.

8. Most strikes are in the private sector.

9. Threat of withdrawal of labour remains a significant part of the trade union negotiating armoury.

10. Shop stewards have a statutory right to reasonable time off to undertake union duties and activities.

Chapter 4:
The MAP and How to Succeed

In chapter 2 we briefly introduced the concept of the MAP as a method of measuring the current status of the working relationship with the trade union. This is a unique model that reflects three key stages of maturity (the traffic lights below) in terms of management and trade union relations. These stages are shown below:

The MAP schematically shows that as relations develop through the three stages of maturity, the underpinning tone of the relationship likewise develops from one of conflict to compromise and ultimately to consensus. We call this the 3 Cs approach.

The MAP then shows the impact the relationship will have on the business performance and graphically demonstrates, as the relationship matures, the likelihood of the relationship yielding a positive impact on the increase in business performance. The business case for partnership is compelling and we will cover this in more detail below.

The Aim of the MAP

The MAP is not intended as a scientific model, rather it is an intuitive model reflective of decades of experience the authors have had in first-hand industrial relations. It also builds on the theory of employee voice and the evidence base that organisations who have engaged workers are more successful than those who do not. Trade unions can be a positive conduit to harness the collective employee voice.

The McCardle and Weightman MAP to Working Positively with Trade Unions

Y-axis: Impact on Performance
X-axis: Maturity of Relationship

The Impact Triangle: Negative → Positive

	Conflict	Compromise	Consensus
	Misalignment	**Acknowledgement**	**Partnership**
Characteristics	• Suspicion • Arrogance • Negativity • Lacking skills • Them & Us • Unstructured • Short-term • Mistrust • Tell • Threats	• Self-Awareness • Understanding • Reflective • Assertive • Willingness • Strengths / Weakness • Challenging • Sell ideas • Cautious	• Respectful • Positive • Thoughtful • Big Picture • Persuasive • Purposeful • Skilled • Openness • Transparent • Joint Problem Solving • Sense of Fairness
	M	A	P

The Business Case for the MAP

Some might argue that managers are paid to manage and of course this is true; the issue is how they manage. No single manager can ever have all the answers or all the best ideas. Successful managers maximise their resources and maximise the collective knowledge and wisdom of those they manage. Ultimately managers are judged on results and they are held to account to deliver these results, sometimes in particularly challenging circumstances.

Successful managers recognise they don't (and can't) know everything. They have self-confidence in their own abilities but acknowledge their limitations and are confident to utilise the skills and contributions of others to augment their own skills and collectively deliver better results. Successful managers respect the trade union as a representative voice of their members. The trade union can be a rich vein of information and intelligence in relation to the feelings of the workforce and are attuned to the needs and aspirations of their members. Trade union representatives can be an effective conduit for the employee voice and a significant asset to the manager if utilised effectively.

Employee voice is about allowing your employees, individually and collectively through their trade union, to express their opinions, concerns and ideas and to enable them to have an influence and meaningful input into work-related decisions.

Where there is a strong employee voice, there are higher levels of engagement. We intuitively know that engaged employees have a greater sense of pride in their work and loyalty to their employer. They go the extra mile and willingly give additional effort, sometimes referred to as discretionary effort, and there is compelling evidence that correlates improved engagement with improved business performance e.g. in terms of:

- Reduced staff turnover
- Greater employee advocacy

- Improved customer satisfaction
- Increased productivity
- Reduced waste
- Increased profit

Ask yourself this: would you rather be cared for by a doctor or nurse who is highly engaged or one who is disengaged with their employer? Would you rather invest your hard-earned savings in a company with engaged workers or disengaged workers? Would you rather go to a restaurant where the staff feel engaged or disengaged?

Clearly there is a compelling case for employee engagement, individually and collectively through trade unions, so what is stopping this happening? Take some time to think about this within your own organisation and list in the table below the things that you think are stopping or hindering employee engagement. Once you have listed these, think about what could be done to help overcome them.

Barriers to Employee Engagement	How Could These Be Overcome
1.	1.
2.	2.
3.	3.
4.	4.
5.	5.

I am sure you will have found that it is easier to identify the barriers but much more difficult to develop solutions. The solutions will take time and will need to be fully considered and discussed with your colleagues at work to gain their support and buy-in.

As we identified in chapter 2, it has long been recognised that collective bargaining through trade unions, properly conducted, is the most effective means of giving workers the right to representation in decisions affecting their working lives. This spirit of employees having an influence on decisions that affect them at work is at the heart of employee voice.

The MAP embraces collective bargaining and embraces the trade union as a valuable collective voice of the workforce. But the MAP goes beyond traditional collective bargaining and extends into wider involvement in areas such as business transformation, quality improvement initiatives and health and wellbeing.

The challenge for organisations, managers and HR practitioners is: how do you achieve this?

The aim of the MAP is to provide you with a practical framework that you can apply in your own workplace, to help you identify what stage your relationship is at, the impact this might be having and to provide a framework to develop these crucial relationships.

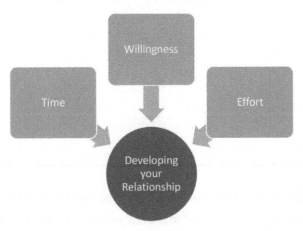

Working Positively with Trade Unions

Progression through the MAP will require commitment and a willingness to change what you do and how you act. It will take time and effort and it may not always be a smooth ride. It will require sustained effort by all parties and sometimes progress might be slow and challenging.

It is important to take some time to look at how effective your relationship is with the trade union and to ensure you are putting your efforts into the right areas. To help your thought process, let us take some time to think about what you believe the characteristics of a successful working relationship with trade unions would look like in your business. Have a go at completing the table below:

Characteristics of a Successful Management / Trade Union Relationship:
1.
2.
3.
4.
5.
6.
7.
8.
9.
10.

That has given you a lot to consider. It may be useful to ask the trade union what they think about your list and even ask them to identify any suitable additions. Think about the characteristics you have identified and see where these would fit on the MAP.

The Three Stages of Development

The MAP identifies three stages of maturity that describe most management / trade union relationships, whether these are at an individual level i.e. between a manager and shop steward, at a departmental or divisional level e.g. between the area management team and Local Consultative Committee (LCC), or at an organisational wide level e.g. which might include directors and senior management and the organisational wide Joint Negating Committee (JNC).

The diagram of the MAP at the beginning of the chapter summarises the typical characterises of the management / union relationship at each of the three stages of maturity. Each stage is expanded on below. As you read through the descriptors think about the relationships with your trade union(s) and later in this chapter we will provide you with a questionnaire that will help you profile where you fit on the MAP.

Stage 1 - Misalignment

Relationships at this stage of the MAP tend to be marred by conflict and negativity. Often this conflict is caused by a misalignment between what the manager wants and what the trade union wants. It is often the case that both sides think they are aligned and understand each other's aims, but when it comes to the crunch, the two simply do not align. Neither side is prepared to accept fault, and simply blame each other. The reality is both are to blame as they have not talked about how they can work effectively together.

This stage of the MAP is often characterised by a degree of arrogance, naivety and / or inexperience. It is common for either the manager or the shop steward to display an attitude of 'I'll tell you' or 'I know best'. It is very much a 'them & us' approach with each side pushing their own agenda, and the general tone is one of resistance and threats e.g. threat of industrial action from the shop steward or threat of imposition by the manager. Some see this as a classic power play where one or both sides seek to assert their strength in the relationship.

It can get fuelled with adrenaline and easily escalate into quite heated dialogue and verbal sparring. I have witnessed on many occasions shop stewards thumping the table with clenched fists, shouting and storming out of meetings. This of course can be just carefully choreographed theatre intended to make some sort of statement, but generally it is more a complete loss of temper. Of course, managers are not immune from this and in any circumstances, this type of behaviour is generally destructive in terms of positive trade union relations and leads to people unwilling to back down and taking up entrenched positions.

Typically, the mindset at this first stage of the MAP is on short-term issues and dealing with the here and now. Tit for tat point scoring is not unusual and it is likely that at least one or both sides will not have undergone any industrial relations training, or their skills in this area will not be particularly well developed. This limits the ability, of either side, to articulate their respective positions to maximum affect and this can quite easily result in discussions and negotiations becoming overly emotive with either side then resorting to 'telling' and making threats to get their points across.

It is not unusual at this stage of the MAP for the manager and trade union representative to display a lot of self-confidence, although possibly misplaced as arrogance or bolshiness, and both will want to make a good impression on their peers. I have seen on numerous occasions shop stewards standing for election and spouting rhetoric of how they will 'get management told this and that' and how they will 'get improvements to this or that terms and conditions'. Likewise, I have seen numerous managers being vocal about how they will sort out the unions or put this or that shop steward in their place. The good thing is that often behind such rhetoric is an enthusiasm and energy.

However, if this energy is not harnessed and used correctly it can easily become destructive and lead to conflict. The reality of this self-confidence and enthusiasm, particularly in newly elected shop stewards or newly promoted managers, may not necessarily be underpinned with the appropriate skills and knowledge to develop the management / trade union relationship to attain the desired stage 3 of the MAP. In these circumstances any positive energy and good intentions are easily misaligned and lose impact. The consequence is management / union relationships in this stage of the MAP are often stormy and marred by conflict. There is little willingness to compromise, and it is very much a one-way street with either side wanting to take but not give.

At this stage of the MAP the manager and / or the shop steward believe their view of the world is all that matters, or that their style is the best way. It is likely the manager will see the trade union as an irritant, blocking them at every twist and turn. The shop steward may well have developed an inherit dislike of management. They may not have had the benefit of experiencing how others negotiate and manage relationships and therefore have no basis to know what works best.

Some relationships never progress beyond this stage and unfortunately many managers and shop stewards still think this is what trade union relations is all about. Some may have never experienced anything else, and may even revel in the conflict, but this can have no place in modern, progressive and productive employee relations. However, the reality is every management / trade union relationship will, at some point, experience some of the characteristics described in the *Misaligned* stage of the MAP.

Even those relationships that successfully develop may, from time to time, regress back.

The important point is to understand and use the MAP to help identify the characteristics of your management / union relationship and identify the factors that positively and negatively affect the relationship with your trade union. This will provide you with the building blocks to develop the relationship and progress through the MAP.

Getting out of the Misalignment stage is often the most challenging part of the MAP. You need to be realistic that progress may be slow at first. There is no silver bullet that will transform your relationship, and progress might not always go smoothly. Even getting to a point of recognising the need for change can be challenging. However, by reading this book you are in a great starting place.

So, before we move, take a few minutes to think about the immediate positive actions you can take to progress your relationship from the Misalignment stage and into Acknowledgement stage of the MAP. Try to list at least 5 actions in the table below. Think also of the things that might hinder or block you and likewise what might aid or assist you. Be realistic; this is about putting in place the foundations to build on. Try to think about the things you can do immediately and over the short term. We will repeat this exercise later in the chapter for the other stages of the MAP, so do not feel you need to change the world in one go.

Actions you could take to move from Misalignment to Acknowledgement	What might stop you?	What would help you?

The actions you have identified need to be practical so that you can easily implement them back at work. If you talk to the trade union, and any others who would be involved e.g. HR, about what you intend to do differently and explain why, you can start to gain their buy-in to the way forward. If you do not share your new ideas, they will be unsure of your motives and may oppose your positive moves.

Stage 2 - Acknowledgement

At this stage the relationship will have developed to a point where both sides start to see beyond the immediate issues and show some willingness to listen to each other's arguments and points of view. Both sides will nonetheless still be quite assertive in their demeanour but adopt a more selling style (as opposed to telling) and their default position of resistance will soften.

Both the manager(s) and the shop steward(s) will have increased their self-awareness and have a greater understanding of the impact their personality, and the approach they adopt, has on the relationship. It is likely both sides will have undergone at least basic training e.g. in discipline and grievance procedures, basic negotiating skills, and effective behaviours, and will be more reflective on the positive and negative impacts they are having on the outcome of the issues they are dealing with. This self-reflection will lead to a moderation or change in behaviour, a bit like a child learning not to fall off the bicycle to avoid the unnecessary pain and injury.

Acknowledgement is a crucial stage in the development of the management/union relationship, as it is an acceptance that neither side is always right, neither has the upper hand and neither has all the answers. Either the manager or the shop steward (or both) will have become more self-aware of their strengths and weaknesses and more reflective of their behaviour and approach to dealing with various issues and will begin to see the merit of compromise and to give and take.

Acknowledgement opens the way for the relationship to be developed and improved and to move the relationship into the third, and most developed, stage of the MAP i.e. Partnership.

Before moving on take a few minutes to think about what actions you could take to progress your relationship further and to progress from Acknowledgement into Partnership, as you did in the previous exercise, try to list at least 5 actions to move you out of Misalignment. Again, list things that might hinder or stop you and the things that would aid or assist you.

Actions you could take to move from Acknowledgement to Partnership	What might stop you?	What would help you?
1.		
2.		
3.		
4.		
5.		

Like the previous exercise, you will need to explain to the trade union what you are trying to do and why it is important. An even better way would be to work together with them in completing the exercise, so together you develop a clear and agreed path forward.

Stage 3 - Partnership

Partnership is the final stage of maturity on the MAP and the ultimate goal. At this stage of the MAP there will be a genuine commitment to work together, in the spirit of trust and cooperation, to deliver solutions and outcomes of mutual benefit to the employer and the workforce.

There will be a mutual respect and both sides will be skilled in negotiating and representing their respective positions on issues. Meetings will generally be constructive, both sides will think through in advance the impact of any given stance they may adopt. This approach is summarised in the diagram below:

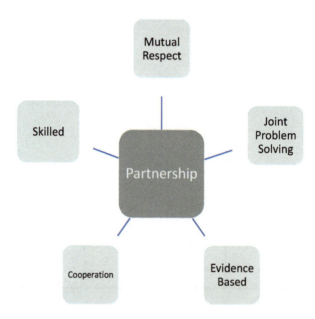

There will be an openness and transparency that is reflective of the trust that has been established. Both sides will be more attuned to the bigger picture, they will seek to persuade one another, rather than overly assert themselves. There will be a spirit of joint problem solving that recognises neither side has the monopoly on the best ideas or knows all the answers. This is not to say either side is a push over - far from it. Both may occasionally have to push their cause and seek to achieve their respective objectives; the key is to have each other's objectives aligned as far as possible. Both sides will be focused on the Recipe for Success we introduced you to in chapter 2 and to keep the scales of power in balance.

Recipe for Success

When true partnership has been achieved, there will be a positive energy and it will feel as if everyone is focused on the same goal and pushing in the same direction.

Problems are anticipated and nipped in the bud. There is an open-door approach, from both sides, and emerging issues will be flagged in confidence to test the water in a spirit of openness and valued opinion. Reasoned, evidence-based argument and persuasion will be the order of the day with a focus on consensus and win-win outcomes.

Occasionally agreement cannot be reached, and respective positions taken, in the worst case, imposition by management and/or industrial action from the trade union. However, this will be rare and a last resort. But, even in these circumstances, the strongest partnerships can survive this. Both sides will have reluctantly accepted the stance taken and understand the consequences of such action. What is telling in well-developed management / trade union relationships at stage 3 of the MAP is the ability of both sides to separate the issue in disagreement and still work positively together in partnership on other matters. They recognise the importance of the relationship and how this must continue, despite the occasional derailment.

Getting to this stage of the MAP will have required considerable effort. Trust will have been hard-earned and can be quickly lost. Both sides need to be alert to any particularly difficult situations and make the necessary investment of effort to ensure the principles of the partnership are maintained. You have previously looked at what action you could take to progress from Misalignment to Acknowledgement and then to Partnership. The key question is: once you are there, what could you do to maintain the partnership?

Take some time to think about this and list the key actions you would take in the box table below:

What action could you take to ensure partnership working is maintained?		
Actions	What might stop you?	What would help you?
1.		
2.		
3.		
4.		
5.		

It is essential that you work at maintaining the current position as it can easily slip backwards. There will always be some little changes you can make to maintain the partnership position and you must not forget to continue the things that got you there!

Where Do You Fit on the MAP?

Now that you know about the MAP and how it is structured, the question is: where do you fit on it?

The questionnaire below has been designed to profile your relationship against the MAP and can be used in a variety of ways e.g. you can complete it individually as a manager, or as a management team; likewise, the shop steward could complete it, or the trade union committee could. You can then compare the results and identify areas where you could improve. Likewise, you can use the questionnaire to profile relationships at different levels within and across your organisation.

During this section we will take you through the questionnaire and provide you with some practical tools and techniques to help you begin to develop your route way to positive and productive management / trade union relations. Each question is scored out of 10, with 1 being low and 10 being excellent. Once the questionnaire is complete there are three ways we can interpret the score:

1. You can simply total up the score and see where this places us on the MAP.
2. You can plot your answers on the profile of the MAP and see the pattern of scores.
3. You can calculate the mean score.

The three scoring options are further explained below, but first let us start with a look at the questionnaire.

MAP Questionnaire

How do you rate your Management /Trade Union relationship?	Score out of 10 (1 = low 10 =high)
1. We understand and respect each other's roles.	
2. Both sides have developed skills and use these effectively.	
3. We avoid getting emotive or letting personality get in the way.	
4. We are adult in our approach to dealing with issues.	
5. We are structured and efficient in our dealings with each other.	
6. We are always consciously trying to improve our relationship.	
7. We handle conflict well together.	
8. There is a willingness from both sides to concede and compromise.	
9. We work well together to deliver a positive future for all.	
10. We welcome different views and challenges.	
11. We sell our ideas to each other.	
12. We trust each other.	
13. We always adopt a joint problem-solving approach.	
14. We keep focused on the big picture.	
15. All relevant information is openly shared.	
Total Score	

Have a go at completing the questionnaire. Don't over think it, remember this is not an exact science. Be honest in your critique, there is no right or wrong answer, it is simply as you see and feel it. Once you have answered all the questions add up your total score.

Now let us have a look at the scoring and how to interpret your results. To help us do this we will use an example of a typical completed questionnaire.

Worked Example

How do you rate your Management /Trade Union relationship?	Score out of 10 (1 = low 10 =high)
1. We understand and respect each other's roles.	6
2. Both sides have developed skills and use these effectively.	4
3. We avoid getting emotive or letting personality get in the way.	4
4. We are adult in our approach to dealing with issues.	6
5. We are structured and efficient in our dealings with each other.	5
6. We are always consciously trying to improve our relationship.	2
7. We handle conflict well together.	2
8. There is a willingness from both sides to concede and compromise.	4
9. We work well together to deliver a positive future for all.	4
10. We welcome different views and challenges.	4

11. We sell our ideas to each other.	4
12. We trust each other.	3
13. We always adopt a joint problem-solving approach.	3
14. We keep focused on the big picture.	4
15. All relevant information is openly shared.	3
Total Score	**58**

Option 1. Total Score

So, what does this score of 58 mean? We can see from the table below this score fits within stage 1 (Misaligned) of the MAP:

Using the total score in this way is a simple and quick way to start assessing where you fit on the MAP. In this example a score of 58 identifies the relationship needs development. It starts to put some objectivity to describing the relationship and gives you a basis to start identifying the areas where you can improve.

Getting the trade union to complete the questionnaire separately and then comparing your results can be highly informative. As mentioned earlier, you can also do this at different levels and you can populate the table below to see the differences in scores.

Comparison of Total Scores

Management Scores	Organisation			
	Department			
	Manager	**58**		
		Shop Steward	LCC	JNC
		Trade Union scores		

LCC = Local Consultative Committee / JCC = Joint Negotiating Committee

Option 2. Score Profile

A more detailed look at the scores by profiling your answers against the MAP will give you a more informed basis to critically look at the relationship and where to start developing your route to a successful and productive relationship. We have taken the scores from the above example and apply them to the profile below:

Let us now take a look at the MAP Profile

Working Positively with Trade Unions

How do you rate your Management /Trade Union relationship?	Misalignment					Acknowledgement			Partnership	
	1	2	3	4	5	6	7	8	9	10
1. We understand and respect each other's roles.						●				
2. Both sides have deveoped skills and use these effectively.				●						
3. We avoid getting emotive or letting personality get in the way.				●						
4. We are adult in our approach to dealing with issues.						●				
5. We are structured and efficient in our dealings with each other.					●					
6. We are always consciously trying to improve our relationship.		●								
7. We handle conflict well together.		●								
8. There is a willingness from both sides to concede and compromise				●						
9. We work well together to deliver a positive future for all.				●						
10. We welcome different views and challenges.				●						
11. We sell our ideas to each other.				●						
12. We trust each other.			●							
13. We always adopt a joint problem-solving approach.			●							
14. We keep focused on the big picture.			●							
15. All relevant information is openly shared.			●							

What we can see from the profile above is that some questions i.e. Q1 and Q4, have scored 6 which places them in the Acknowledged stage of development whereas the rest are in the red zone and some i.e. Q1 and Q13 score particularly low with scores of just 2. These variations are easily overlooked when using the total score in isolation.

Now plot your own scores on the MAP profile (blank template is available in Appendix 7). What areas do you score best and weakest? By comparing your profile against the trade unions, you will be able to identify any areas of commonality and any major differences.

The aim is to have as many dots (scores) as possible as far to the right of the MAP as possible and to have your scores aligned in as many cases as you can with trade union. The scores must be honest to get the best results.

Option 3. Mean Score

The third way to show your scores is by using a mean score and score range. Using our example of the completed questionnaire above, we show how to calculate the mean score below:

		Misalignment				Acknowledgement			Partnership		
A	Score	1	2	3	4	5	6	7	8	9	10	Total
B	Frequency	0	2	3	7	1	2	0	0	0	0	15
C	Total Score / Q	0	4	9	28	5	12	0	0	0	0	58
D	Mean Score						3.9					

How to calculate the mean score:

A = the score available for each question

B = the number of questions you have given this score to e.g. you can see from the example questionnaire that two questions were scored 2, three questions scored 3, etc.

C = A x B

D = the Total Score divided by the Total Frequency i.e. 58 ÷ 15 = 3.9

Note the total frequency should always be 15 i.e. the same as the number of questions in the MAP Questionnaire. If more than one person is completing the questionnaire then this will be multiples of 15 e.g. for two people if will be 30, for three completing the questionnaire it will add up to 45, etc.

Using the mean score option works particularly well when using the questionnaire in groups as it allows you to input the data into a spreadsheet format as in the above example and it will easily produce a mean score for the group easily. You will also be able to see the range of scores across the group of people who have completed the questionnaire.

If you find there is a wide variation from the lowest to the highest score this will show a wide difference of views within the group. This would be a good area to explore e.g. to find out what experiences are shaping people's view of the relationship.

The aim is to get the mean score as high as possible and to have the range of scores within the group as narrow as you can i.e. so that as many of the group are thinking the same. Because the mean score is a basic statistical calculation out of a maximum of ten, it is very easy then to equate how well you are doing against the MAP e.g. a mean score less than 5 is in Misalignment, a score of 6 to 8 is in Acknowledgement, whereas a score of 9 or 10 is in Partnership. In the work example above, we instantly know 3.9 (or 39%) is within the Misalignment stage of the MAP.

An extension of this option is to calculate the group mean score by each of the 15 questions. A worked example based on real scores from a European Works Council is attached in Appendix 8.

Irrespective of which scoring option suits you best, and you could use all three, it is important to remember the score is simply to help you focus your efforts on what you can do to develop your relationship with the trade union and help you progress through the MAP. Once you have completed the questionnaire and determined your score, it will give you a base line to periodically monitor your progress against and reflect on the positive progress you are making.

A Route to Success

A good way of formalising your commitment to developing your relationship with your trade union is to produce a plan. Some organisations call this their Partnership Agreement, some refer to it as their Statement of Intent, others refer to it as their Employee Relations Framework.

To help you get started we have set out below a Five Point guide for you to follow. Remember to reflect on the exercises you have done and use these to input into your plan. Some organisations have a 'formal' signing of the plan together with their trade union partners and this can be a symbolic and positive message to the rest of the workforce.

Five Point Plan to Success

1. Aims & Objectives
2. Values & Principles
3. Critical Success Factors
4. Barriers & Aids
5. Process & procedures

Partnership Agreement

Working through the five-point plan together, particularly through a series of facilitated workshops, can prove particularly beneficial. This process itself will significantly help you develop your relationship. As you work through the plan, reflect on where you are on the MAP and think about the various exercises you have completed to identify the actions to move you forward, the things you will need to overcome as you progress and the things that will assist you to do this.

Point 1. Agree the Aims and Objectives of the Partnership

It is essential the aims and objectives of the partnership are developed together. This may sound like a statement of the obvious, but it is not unusual for management to write these and then present them to the trade union and expect them to agree them. Of course, it can be unnerving for management to start with an open book and enter a process of agreeing a set of objectives, especially if you are currently rooted in stage 1 – Misalignment, on the MAP.

However, there must be some leaps of faith, there must be a genuine commitment (from both management and trade union representatives) to work in partnership. The aims and objectives set out what the partnership is seeking to achieve and provide a basis against which to assess the success of the partnership at staged intervals.

The aims and objectives should be aspirational, but like other business objectives, these should be realistic and attainable, otherwise they will have little credibility and will simply set the partnership up to fail. They should describe the purpose of the plan and what you are trying to achieve.

Point 2. Agree the Values and Principles That All Partners Will Stick To.

Values and principles are crucial to guide the interaction between managers and shop stewards. They are normally a reflection of the aspiration for the wider organisational culture. These values and principles set the tone. They are the yardstick by which to hold each other to account.

The easy thing is writing them, the hard bit is living and breathing them. The reality might be that the current values by which managers and trade unions are conducting their business may be very different from those that are aspired from the partnership. Values and principles e.g. challenge without conflict, mutual trust and respect, etc. only have any worth if they have integrity, which in simple words means doing as you say.

Point 3. Identify the Critical Success Factors That Will Enable the Partnership to Flourish.

Having established the bedrock for the relationship, the next step is to jointly identify the critical success factors i.e. the things that are crucial to enabling the relationship to develop and thrive. Once you have identified and agreed your critical success factors, you need to commit these into action i.e. what – when – how - who. Critical success factors should be kept under review and if circumstances change they should be amended or changed.

Point 4. Identify the Barriers That Will Inhibit the Partnership.

Barriers can easily be confused with critical success factors, but they are different. Critical success factors are more about the main things that will enable the relationship to grow and develop. Barriers are the things that will stop or hinder the relationship developing. Nullifying a barrier might not in itself be a critical success factor. However, what barriers do have in common with critical success factors is they must also be committed to action and kept under regular review.

Point 5. Agree the Process of Joint Working.

The final stage of the five-point plan is to agree the actual process, the mechanics, of how the relationship will function. This could involve e.g. meeting structure and frequency, approach to joint problem solving, decision making, communications, conflict resolution, etc. It can be useful to document these processes and procedures to help ensure the effective administration of the partnership. You should also agree how the relationship will be periodically reviewed, including how and when you will review where you fit against the MAP.

Key Points

1. Workforce engagement equals business success.
2. Engagement means listening to, involving and valuing employees.
3. Trade unions represent the collective voice of the workforce.
4. Trade unions can be positive advocates for change and innovation.
5. Solutions must fair, affordable and sustainable.
6. There must be a balance of power and shared benefits.
7. All too often management /trade union relationships are marred by conflict.
8. Relationships need time, effort and commitment to make them work.
9. Relationships are built on a foundation of trust, mutual respect and fairness.
10. The MAP provides the basis to develop your route MAP to success.

Chapter 5:
Building Engagement with Trade Unions

Introduction

In the previous chapter we introduced you to the MAP that describes three key stages of maturity covering all management and trade union relationships. We have provided you with the MAP questionnaire as a tool to identify where you fit on the MAP and introduced you to a number of exercises to help you develop a route map to develop positive working relationships with trade unions.

In this chapter we will expand further on the importance of individual relationships with the trade union

Who Do You Engage with the Trade Union?

We briefly covered how trade unions are structured in chapter 3 and in general terms the most pivotal trade union role is the shop steward. There are approximately 200,000 shop stewards representing members in the workplace throughout the UK, and when we talk about working with trade unions, many people think about the shop steward representing members at disciplinary hearings, helping members pursue grievances or pursuing members' rights to certain terms and conditions.

However, the role of the shop steward is much more than this and, particularly in larger organisations, some of the activities of the shop steward are undertaken by other elected trade union representatives e.g. the Union Learning Representative (ULR) and the trade union Health & Safety representative. Some trade unions also have Equalities & Diversity and Environmental representatives, although it should be noted these particular roles are not entitled to statutory facility time.

These trade union representatives often become expert in their designated field and can add real value to the workplace e.g. there is extensive evidence to show that involvement of trade union Health and Safety representatives helps reduce injuries at work and leads to reductions in the levels of ill-health caused by work. The TUC are an excellent source of further information on the evidence base for active trade union involvement in workplace health and safety.

Similarly, there is compelling evidence that a skilled workforce is more efficient and productive and helps deliver real bottom line results. Workers are having to constantly learn new skills and embrace new technology and new ways of working. This can be daunting for some people and many workers become adept at masking their lack of skill or fear of learning new skills. Trade unions are attuned to these fears and help address these concerns. The TUC estimate that trade unions, through ULRs, help over 230,000 people take up learning every year.

It is important to distinguish the various roles the trade union reps undertake. Even if all the roles are being undertaken by the shop steward, it is still important to know when he/she is fulfilling which element of the role. This is important because it helps to contextualise workplace issues and shapes how we interact with the trade union. Ordinarily issues of workplace learning will be less contentious than e.g. a disciplinary hearing for serious misconduct. But we often see issues conflated, particularly in relationships at stage 1 of the MAP, and a perception forms that everything is difficult to deal with.

We will cover dealing with difficult situations in more detail later in chapter 12, but first let us consider a typical structure of management / trade union relationships. The previous chapter described the MAP and explained how relationships with the trade union can vary at different levels and in different areas of the business. At the heart of these relationships are people, often the manager and the shop steward. But there are other key relationships, and we have summarised below what a typical framework of management / trade union relationships looks like in a medium to large size business.

Level	Local Unit level		Business Unit level		Organisation level		
Focus	Here and Now		Medium term		Long term		
Who	Supervisor	Manager	HR Manager	Department Head	Operations Director	HR Director	Chief Executive
Shop Stewards	x	x	x	x	x	x	
H&S representatives	x	x	x	x	x		
TU Learning representatives	x	x	x	x			
Joint Consultative Committee			x	x	x	x	x
Joint Negotiating Committee				x	x	x	
Full-Time Officer			x	x	x	x	x
National Officers					x	x	x

Of course, every organisation is different and the nature and size of your business will shape the structure of your involvement, and therefore your relationship with, the trade union.

In a large organisation you may be dealing with multiple trade unions, with many trade union representatives operating over multiple sites, whereas in a small business you may be dealing with just one trade union, with only one or two reps in one location. The table above is a basic representation of the types of management and trade union interactions and begins to highlight the complexity of trade union relations across an organisation.

Shop Steward

Relationships at the local level tend mainly to be between the shop steward (and ULRs and H&S reps where these roles are separated) and the supervisor and/or line manager and will typically deal with issues that arise on a day to day basis. However, the very same reps will also deal with the middle management e.g. the department or function head and HR on the more ongoing type issues e.g. the level of investment for skills development, safety plans, shift patterns, sickness absence, etc. Likewise, the same shop stewards may deal with senior management e.g. the Operations and HR Directors on the longer term and strategic issues e.g. to discuss H&S trends, workforce trends, skills shortages, positive action campaigns to improve workforce diversity, etc.

Due to this level of involvement across a wide range of the business, the shop steward often has greater knowledge and understanding of the business than the supervisor and line managers they are engaging with and this can lead to resentment.

It is unlikely shop stewards will have general direct dealing with the Chief Executive. However, it is quite common for the Chief Executive to periodically meet with shop stewards, sometimes through the Joint

Consultative Committee, to discuss the big picture issues e.g. how the business is performing, its future direction, emerging issues e.g. Brexit. In one organisation I worked for these briefings were affectionately referred to as 'state of the nation' briefings.

Interestingly, the government similarly engages with trade unions and will have briefings with the TUC and trade union general secretaries at a national level. Governments, like successful businesses, recognise that the trade unions represent a significant section of the UK workforce and are key stakeholders in the employment landscape.

Shop stewards, or a smaller representative group of them, will form the Joint Negotiating Committee (JNC) and collectively bargain on behalf of their members, and those non-union members who also form part of the bargaining unit, with senior management e.g. the Operations and HR Directors, will normally represent the management side.

Significance of the Full-Time Officer

The full-time trade union officers (FTOs) have an influential role in the overall management / trade union relationship. Sometimes the FTOs sit on the JNC and they will often get involved in more complex cases e.g. a contested dismissal, individual or collective equal pay claims, bullying cases. Shop stewards have the right of representation by their FTO e.g. if they are personally involved in a disciplinary action. It is common place for full-time officers to be involved in annual pay negotiations.

Full-time officers normally represent members across several different businesses and have the benefit of being more emotionally detached from the organisation e.g. they are less likely to get caught up in personality clashes. They are generally skilled negotiators and have expertise in matters of employment law. They can bring a sense of perspective and see issues though a different lens, often suggesting an alternative course of action, and generally focus on positive resolution.

Full-time officers can be a useful sounding board, particularly if you are having difficulty with a shop steward. Of course, the FTO is there to support their shop stewards, but I have experienced on several occasions the skilful way they have subtly used their experience and influence to moderate the attitude or behaviours of the shop steward.

What Do We Engage About?

Irrespective of the size and nature of your business, your relationship with the trade union will be influenced by a wide range of issues. These issues can be categorised broadly into three groups:

1. Issues that need immediate attention e.g. there might be a staffing issue on the shop floor or in the office.
2. Issues that require attention and resolution over a period of weeks and months (medium term) e.g. this might be in relation to varying work patterns to meet peaks in operational demand.
3. Issues that will have a long-term impact such as pay, business restructuring, etc.

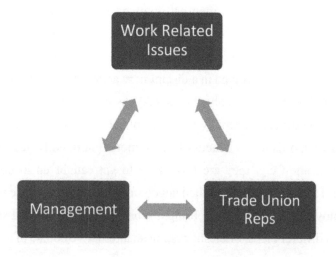

Some of the issues will be individual and some will be collective, some will be relatively straight forward, and some will be complex. Let us take some time to think about the types of issues on which you engage with the trade union in your organisation.

Complete the table below and identify the types of issues that are relevant to individual workers e.g. an appeal against a flexible working request being declined, as well as those issues that affect collective groups e.g. a pay negotiation. Try to split the issues between those that are relatively straightforward compared to those that are more complex.

	Types of Issues	
	Straightforward	**Complex**
Individual	1. 2. 3. 4.	1. 2. 3. 4.
Collective	1. 2. 3. 4.	1. 2. 3. 4.

How these issues are dealt with influences the relationship with the trade union, but then the nature of the relationship can equally influence how they are dealt with. A chicken and egg situation, one might say. Furthermore, what is straightforward in one organisation or in one part of an organisation might be complex to another. Likewise, what might be a straightforward issue to resolve with one trade union might be complex with another.

Understanding this complexity will help you understand how your relationship with the trade union operates and how it might be improved.

Profile of Engagement

Let us expand on the issues you have identified above and think about the trade union relationships you have in your business and how these relationships impact on the issues on which you are engaging with the trade union.

Start by taking the issues you identified in the exercise above and use these to complete the table below. For each issue identify who, from both the management and the trade union side, are normally involved in dealing with these issues. It is quite possible that you may deal with the same individual(s) on many or all the issues, but the relationship, and how well you deal with these, can vary significantly. Therefore, to help get a better understanding of this, against each issue you have listed, tick whether these issues generally get well managed or whether they could be improved.

Completing the table in this way will help profile the type of issues you have to deal with and what is working well and help you focus on where there are opportunities to further develop your relationship with the trade union.

Let's look at engagement

	Who is Involved?		How Effectively are These Issues Managed?	
Typical Issues	Management side	Trade Union side	Good	Could be better
Straightforward issues *Individual:* 1. 2. 3. 4. *Collective:* 1. 2. 3. 4.				
Complex issues *Individual:* 1. 2. 3. 4. *Collective:* 1. 2. 3. 4.				

Remember it is important to build on the things that are working well and to identify actions on which you might improve, in those areas where you have identified they could be managed better. Build these actions into your 5 Point Plan we discussed in chapter 4.

Think about what it is that is making a difference between those things that work well compared to those where you could improve. Think about what is causing this and identify actions to help you improve. Think about who you need to involve in this process and try and get their collective buy-in to the improvement actions. Invite the views of the trade union; they will probably have some good ideas to help improve the level of engagement.

The Emotional Bank Account

There is an old saying 'fix the roof when the sun is shining' and this is true of trade union relations. Successful relationships are built on a foundation of trust, mutual respect, a willingness to give and take.

Foundations of Successful Relationships

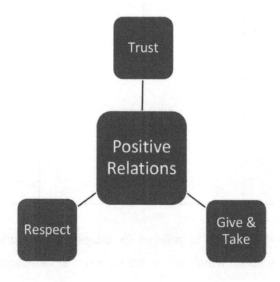

We know from previous chapters that establishing these foundations takes time, willingness and effort. I recall attending a Train the Trainer event more than 30 years ago and being introduced to the concept of the emotional bank account. I immediately recognised a wider application for this and have successfully applied this concept to developing positive trade union relationships over many years.

The emotional bank account works on the same basic principles of your own private bank account i.e. you have to make deposits before you can make a withdrawal; it is good to stay in a positive balance, and only on rare occasions should you overdraw.

You can use the emotional bank account to help build the foundations for a positive trade union relationship. But why should the trade union trust you? And why should you trust them? Well, someone must start somewhere, and it is for management to lead this process and to open the emotional bank account. This means opening the account up with some initial deposits, and thereafter keeping the account topped up.

Try and identify some things you can improve, invest in or change that will be acknowledged by the trade union e.g. improve locker facilities, provide some additional training, upgrade the printer in the trade union office, etc. These need not be high value, but ideally will be visible and symbolic of your willingness to make some investment in the relationship.

Take a few minutes to think about what early deposits you could make to your emotional bank account and list these in the table below:

Things I could do to build my emotional bank balance
1.
2.
3.
4.
5.

It is quite possible during your regular dialogue with the trade union they might push you for x or y. In these circumstances you could consider making some concessions. However, you should let the trade union know you don't have to do this. As a gesture to show your commitment to building a positive relationship with the trade union, make it known you are prepared to give on this or that. In doing this you are making it clear you are prepared to be flexible and willing to work positively with the trade union.

I have found it helpful to meet with trade union reps and explain my approach to trade union relations. I explain that I appreciate they want the best for their members but make it clear that I also want the best I can for my employees i.e. in this respect we have the same common goal. I then explain it is simply a case of what is fair, affordable and sustainable i.e. the recipe for success.

You should always be aware of when you are making a deposit into the emotional bank account and make it known that you are doing so. Of course, this requires some subtly and sincerity; it can even be communicated with a bit of humour.

I then explain what I consider the foundations for a successful relationship and acknowledge that I will have to gain their trust, and likewise they will have to gain mine. I seek their views and suggest we agree some basic grounds rules on how we will operate together. I am clear, from the onset, that on some occasions they will want or need a concession from me and likewise at some point I may need one from them. Many of the situations you and the trade union deal with are rarely clear cut and generally have a degree of discretion that can be legitimately applied. The more the relationship matures the more this give and take will be respected.

By setting out and agreeing expectations in a positive dialogue with the reps, this means that when I do make a concession I can remind them I am giving something i.e. making a deposit in the emotional bank account, and gently remind them I may need a concession at some time. A little bit of humility can go a long way. It is important for both sides to understand the relationship is a two-way process. This willingness to compromise is a key characteristic of stage 2 of the MAP.

Opening the emotional bank account can be a big step in helping you move from stage 1 – Misalignment to stage 2 – Acknowledgement of the MAP. The more you grow your bank balance, the more trust and respect will build and when you do need a concession i.e. need to make a withdrawal, the easier this should be.

Opening the emotional bank account is just one step, and to fully embed a relationship of trust and mutual respect, you need to engage the trade union. We discussed in the previous chapter that for this engagement to be meaningful the trade union e.g. the shop steward and/or full-time officer must feel their views and opinions are valued, they must have the opportunity to influence and help shape the relationship and feel they are being seriously listened to.

Let us pause to enable you to reflect on the level of engagement you have with the trade union and to think about how this engagement could be improved. List the things you could do to improve the level of engagement with the trade union in the table below. Think about the different interaction you have with the trade union and whether you need to adopt different actions e.g. in relation to how you improve engagement with the full-time officer compared to the shop steward.

Action to improve level of TU Engagement	How Easy to Implement?		
	Easy	Moderate	Difficult
1.	•	•	•
2.	•	•	•
3.	•	•	•
4.	•	•	•
5.	•	•	•

Once you have listed the things you could do to improve the level of engagement with the trade union, rate how difficult each action will be to implement. Remember, building positive relationships takes time and this should be considered a marathon not a sprint. Bag the easy wins and plan out how you will progress the more challenging improvement actions. Remember it is easier to build relationships when you are not in conflict.

Food for Thought

Every relationship, and every organisation, is of course different and what works for one may or may not work for another. Likewise, the actions you take to improve the level of engagement, and hence the strength of the relationship, with the trade union will depend on where your relationship currently fits on the MAP e.g. if you are rooted in stage 1, it is unlikely you would have the trust and confidence in the trade union to invite them to sit on the Management Board.

We have listed below some ideas for you to think about, but what matters most is what will work for you:

- Create forums for the trade union to put ideas forward e.g. to improve staff morale, improve efficiency, improve quality, etc.
- Involve the trade union in the corporate induction programme for new starters.
- Put out joint management and trade union communications in good times, and not just when you are dealing with difficult situations.
- Involve the trade union as partners in joint problem solving.
- Float ideas past the trade union e.g. to test the water, in confidence if appropriate. Only by taking shop stewards and full-time officers into your confidence will trust grow.
- Brief the trade union reps regularly and keep them informed and updated about the business. This avoids shocks and surprises and helps build a sense of shared ownership.
- Proactively invite the trade union to share their concerns and aspirations.
- Consciously change the language you use, talk regularly about partnership, sharing ideas, engagement, win–win outcomes, etc.
- Keep in touch with the full-time officers and keep them sighted. Highlight potential problem issues early to them.
- Develop your own understanding of issues affecting the trade union e.g. their local, regional and national elections.

- Attend the trade union branch AGM (if invited) to demonstrate that your commitment to partnership working is real. Your attendance or that of senior executives is a very symbolic gesture that you value the trade union. The AGM gives you a good insight into the issues members are raising with their elected representatives; this can be enlightening.
- Do not be mean on the amount of facility time. You can go beyond the statutory minimum requirement. Think of it as a deposit into the emotional bank account.
- Arrange joint management and trade union training and team building events.
- Ensure the trade unions have good facilities in the workplace.
- Arrange joint social events and have regular informal catch ups.
- Invite the trade union to be represented on management boards / committees / working groups. I have seen this work brilliantly.

Mutual Benefit

You want to succeed as a manager and the shop steward and full-time officer also want to succeed in their roles. There are many opportunities for you to support one another to succeed with legitimacy and integrity. Ultimately, your greatest opportunity for mutual success is by developing your relationship to stage 3 of the MAP and to work genuinely in partnership.

I recall a very personal example of how the trust I had developed with the full-time officer helped me. The business had displaced the trade union branch secretary in a restructuring of the department he worked in. He was a very long-serving employee and trade union rep and he was renowned as a blocker and resistive to just about any change. This had no bearing on the reason for the restructure (he was a technically able employee), but it serves to highlight the extra difficulty this brought to the situation. Allegations of victimisation on the grounds of trade union involvement were put forward and the whole situation became increasingly complex.

I had involved the FTO from the onset in the case and had over many years built a trusted working relationship with her. The branch secretary had become intransigent and the case was heading to the Employment Tribunal. The FTO made a good case for a settlement agreement and I agreed to go down this route. I was under significant pressure from my Chief Executive to resolve this matter before I went off on annual leave and I hit an impasse with the individual just a couple of days before my leave. Pressure on me was mounting from my Chief Executive who was not being particularly supportive or helpful in the matter.

Then out of the blue I got a call from the FTO saying she knew I was going off on leave with my family and knew the pressure I was being put under to resolve the case. She went on to tell me 'off the record' that the she was of the view the offer I had made was more than fair and if the branch secretary remained intransigent and insisted on taking the case to the ET, the trade union would not be

> supporting the individual and that I should go off on holiday and not worry about the case.
>
> She didn't have to do that. She did it unsolicited and acknowledged the fairness of the offer, appreciated I had responded to her suggestion of a settlement agreement and had fully involved him in an open and transparent way throughout. She also recognised the importance of sustaining the positive relationship beyond this case. I had reached my maximum negotiating position and had nowhere else to go (other than the Employment Tribunal) and she believed and trusted me.
>
> I went off on leave in a much more relaxed state and by the time I got back the full-time officer had resolved the issues with the branch secretary and a signed agreement was on my desk. She didn't say it, and she didn't need to, but I had just benefited from a withdrawal from the emotional bank account!

Use the MAP to Review and Monitor Your Progress

It is important to remember the trade unions are the voice of their members, they can be an excellent barometer of the mood and of the workforce attuned to their needs and expectations. Trade unions can be a rich source of workforce intelligence and can help identify and nip issues in the bud.

They can be a source of innovation and advocates of change to benefit both the employer and their members. Your relationship with the trade union is crucial to yielding these positive impacts. By developing positive working relationships with the trade union you are increasing your probability of achieving mutual success and shared benefits.

Remember to use the MAP to periodically profile trade unions relations across your organisation and at different levels e.g. between the manager and the shop steward and between the manager and the FTO. Review the actions you have taken and monitor the progress you are making against the MAP and the positive impact this is having on the business.

As we highlighted earlier, the shop steward is a pivotal role within the trade union and therefore often front and centre of the management / trade union relationship. We will look at this specific aspect of trade union relations in more detail in the next chapter.

Key Points

1. Shop stewards play a pivotal role in the trade union structure.
2. Some trade union duties are undertaken by dedicated roles e.g. Trade Union Learning and Health & Safety reps, and they can add real bottom line value to the business.
3. The complexity of trade union relationships within an organisation can easily be underestimated.
4. Shop stewards (or work place representatives) are front and centre in this relationship.
5. Full-time trade union officers (FTOs) can play an influential role in helping to deliver success.
6. Trust, mutual respect and compromise are at the heart of positive relationships between management and trade unions.
7. Valuing the views and opinions of the trade union, seriously listening to them and meaningfully involving them in joint problem solving will help build trust and mutual respect.

8. Open an emotional bank account to help you build and maintain positive trade union relations.
9. Incorporate the improvement actions you have identified into your 5 Point Plan for Success.
10. Use the MAP to review and monitor your progress.

Chapter 6:
The Role of the Line Manager

Have you ever heard a line manager moan about their team, saying "They are not interested in what we as a management team say, they only listen to the shop steward"? Unfortunately, this is something I have heard far too often over the years. It is a regular saying and is usually born out of frustration by a manager or supervisor not being able to influence their team when it really matters.

This may be a real frustration, but the root cause I have always found to be is the line manager. The line manager has probably failed to act in a consistent manner in the past and failed to own previous communications. It is likely they have taken the easy way out and not bothered to make an effort to take control of communications. In some cases they feel they can't do it and in others they don't want to do it.

I am sure we can all recognise at least one person like that in our own organisation. We can see the problem they have caused but they blame the receivers of the communications as the root of the problem. Until they can see that they have been part of the problem, they cannot be helped. They are happy to blame their team as it is an easy option. They fail to see that it is their responsibility to ensure the team listen to what is important and they need to change their style of delivery if it is not working.

Such people generally seem to think that the shop steward has an influence over the workforce, therefore the team listen and act as instructed by the shop steward. It may be the case, but only because you have given the shop steward the gap in information which they are quite capable of filling. Once the shop steward is seen to regularly fill the gap, it is very difficult for the line manager to take back the necessary control they have relinquished.

The line manager has lost the initiative and interest of the group and this is probably recognised by the workforce. The worst managers I have met seem to believe the workforce should be self-motivated and be able to read minds. They seem to believe that the workforce should know what is required of them without being told. They want an easy ride and expect their team to make things happen when required. Unfortunately, life is not so easy and only those who put in the effort will gain the rewards they all would welcome.

Those line managers who put in the effort to engage, inform and motivate their teams tend to have less negative transactions with their shop stewards. These people are usually operating at stage 3 of the MAP, or close to it. The line managers who do not make a positive effort will inevitably have a more difficult and negative interface with their local shop stewards. These people will generally be at stage 1 of the MAP and will see that as the only option, as any progress will require hard work, determination and application.

Good managers will usually have good shop stewards. They will work together to achieve the business goals whilst ensuring the workforce are looked after. This leads to the building of respect and trust. When respect and trust are high, a good shop steward will ensure they do not take issues up directly with the line manager unless the individuals have seen their line manager first.

So, it is worth looking at what good managers do to ensure they have a positive effect on their team and the local shop steward - this can help you identify good practices that offer a positive reward for all the team and build positive relationships that are built on solid ground.

If you act in a positive manner and do the right things to engage your team, a shop steward can only support what you are doing as you are leaving little room for negative activities. The shop steward will only have to deal with anomalies that may happen from time to time. They will not be involved in regular discipline or grievance cases as the team will be positively motivated. This is a good position for both parties. You can achieve this by applying yourself to a few basic principles that will require time and effort but will offer positive results.

Line Manager's Role.

It is the line manager's role to manage their team to achieve specific objectives that will enhance the success of the organisation. This is not an easy job and requires a lot of applied effort to ensure that success happens.

Line managers generally have two main roles. They have to develop a complement between the process side of their role and the people management aspect of the job. The process side of the role involves dealing with procedures and equipment as well as administration. This may not be easy, but it has a logical pattern that can be simply followed. The people side of the role requires skill and application to gain success.

This is where some line managers abdicate their responsibility as it may be hard at times. As a result, the shop steward will fill the void left by a lazy manager. Hence the frustration of the line manager comes from their own lack of actions with the team on a regular basis. They have abdicated the people side of the role but still want to have control of their team when it is required to help them achieve their objectives.

Working Positively with Trade Unions

Line Manager's Role

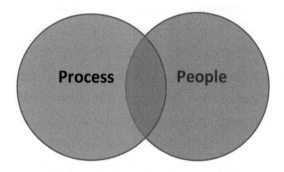

If you look at what good managers do with their teams and their shop stewards, you can set up a way to copy the good practices and hopefully gain the benefits that you desire.

Good line managers:

- Regularly communicate what they require from the team.
- Set targets or goals so there is a clear focus to what needs to be achieved.
- Offer regular feedback to show how the team and individuals are performing.
- Regularly communicate and motivate the team.
- Share their goals so everyone is aware of where their efforts fit into the big picture.

None of the above can happen without a considered and concerted effort on the part of the line manager. This is what may take time but it is what gets you the ongoing results and consistency you require. You may think that we have left the shop steward out of this process but this person is one of your team and needs to have the same positive treatment that the others expect. By acting in a proactive and positive way you are building a relationship with everyone including the shop steward.

By leading the team and regularly motivating the individuals, you can achieve engagement by the workforce with the organisation's objectives. This cannot happen if the individuals in the team are unaware of the organisation's objectives and how the organisation is performing.

This leadership role is important and comes with the responsibility to set time aside to engage with the team in order to gain the necessary level of commitment. The time allocated to this will vary with the organisation and the role. However, it involves a daily commitment of talking to the team and the individuals. Without the commitment from the leader the team will seek an alternative leader. Step in the natural new leader, the shop steward who may not even want the role.

I worked with a great line manager early in my career. This person was highly regarded by the team and by other managers. They got things done but the tasks never seemed impossible. We all liked what we did and got a high level of job satisfaction from what we did. At the time we regarded the situation as normal.

When this person was promoted, our new manager was very different. It was at this stage we realised how good our previous manager had been. They were actively involved in what we did and always had time to chat about what we were doing. If we were struggling or made mistakes, we were coached and encouraged to make improvements. We never faced any anger or ire. This person was fair but equally demanding of our best efforts.

The greatest strength they had was their communication skills. They made everything live and seem achievable. They had time for everyone and were great at listening to ideas, even if they were not so great.

The best trait the person had was that we all wanted to be like him. We wanted to involve people and communicate well. This person showed us how it is done naturally, so much so that a lot of their good points were difficult to replicate as we found it difficult to identify just what they had done. We knew we always felt motivated, but most of us could not identify exactly what had created that feeling. It is only years later you can identify what was done.

I am sure we all want to do a good job, but do we always apply the correct level of effort into the role? We must ask ourselves: 'What is our level of commitment to our job and the team?' On a daily basis we need to:

1. Brief the team about the day ahead.
2. Walk the job at least twice a day.
3. Talk to each team member regularly.
4. Offer regular feedback on performance to the team and individuals.

None of this is easy; however, it is essential to retain the lead role in the group and manage the team effectively. Knowing what makes a difference allows you to put in the right amount of time to get the best results.

Activity Log

Why not look at yourself and establish what you are doing and what you need to do with your team, and the amount of time you allocate to this important part of the role? Establish how much time you are setting aside for the engagement of the team as well as the shop steward. Over a one-week period, keep a log of what time you spend on each area of your commitment. This will help you identify what you need to do to be more effective and what you should keep doing.

Activity	Time				
	1	2	3	4	5
Daily Brief					
Walk the Job 1					
Walk the Job 2					

Time with Individuals					
Feedback					
Shop Steward					

Such a log shows the reality of what you do at work which is so easy to take for granted. It takes a little time to keep the log and ensure it is accurate. When completed you need to see what needs to improve and offer an action plan to improve. You will now have a route forward. Without the route forward you will remain static and possibly go backwards. Always look at the areas you have done well and identify how you will maintain that position.

Let us look at the areas you need to work with in order to get the results you need to engage your team. The areas sound easy to do, but to do them justice you need to not just take the actions but perform them in the right way. By doing this you will get the end result you require. If you pay lip service to this area you will get poor results and increased frustration from the team and this may lead to the shop steward's involvement in areas of your control due to your lack of efforts.

You may be wondering why we are looking at how to manage and communicate with the workforce instead of looking at the shop steward's relationship. The reason for this is that you cannot form an effective relationship with the shop steward if you are not managing your team. If you abdicate the management of people you will create an environment where someone else or a shop steward can thrive in what is essentially your role. This is not fair on the shop steward or the workforce.

Regular Brief

If you have a regular effective form of communication you can avoid the issue of the team not being aware of the department goals and the progress that is being made. This is an integral part of the process of engagement but requires effort to do it right and get positive results.

Anyone can read a brief to a team. This is pure one-way communication which is not overly effective. One needs to have a content that is relevant to the audience and it needs to be delivered in a two-way manner to get and retain interest. Without interest, the brief will be seen as dry and not relevant to the audience and they will switch off. Remember it is you that has made them switch off by your lack of effort.

Whatever the content of the brief, you must keep asking yourself:

- Why am I telling the audience this?
- What does it mean to the team and individuals?
- What do I want the team to do with the information?

If you cannot answer these question before you deliver a brief, don't brief it as you will find that the team will show a lack of interest. If you are unsure of the content, find out the details in advance so that the correct information is being used.

The area of 'What does it mean to the group?' is important as the line manager should be explaining the content of the brief in a manner that the group understands. The key issues of the organisation and how it affects them and their role need to be highlighted when necessary. It will help individuals in your team understand where their efforts support the business goals. This is a way to gain buy-in and commitment. The group needs to know how any content in the brief affects them and their role.

A typical brief format for a manufacturing company is outlined below.

Basic actions
    Start
    Good morning/afternoon
    This brief will last… minutes
    Check head count is correct to ensure all are present
    Check that the team are wearing correct safety clothing (visual check)

Content:

Safety
    Safety principle of the day
    Any accidents in department in the last 24 hours
    Any accidents on specific line (other departments) in the last 24 hours

Customer quality concerns
    Quality concerns raised on specific lines in the last 24 hours
    What is the 5S action for the day (activity to keep the work area safe and tidy)

Site brief Items

General information brief

Actions from the brief
    Summary of key actions for the shift/week
    Ask for any relevant questions
    Thank the team

The above shows the typical content of the brief. This is easy to collate as it is a regular and in some cases a daily update. You can keep the team updated by making it a two-way process. You can ask about any quality or safety concerns they may have. This shows both your interest in and commitment to the issues that matter to the group. Ensure you follow up any items that are raised and report back to the team to show you value their input. Failure to do this will show a lack of interest on your part and will lead to less involvement in the communications process by the team in the future.

If you have failed to brief effectively in the past, it is no excuse to continue in that way. You may wish to talk to your shop steward to explain why you are going to re-commence the briefing and seek their input. By listening and taking actions on the advice you will get the necessary level of support you need to make the re-launch a success.

When starting again:

- You can ask the team what they feel they need to know.
- What items would they want to see included in the brief in the future?
- Explain to the team what you will do differently.
- Ask them for feedback on the content and delivery.
- They will prefer an effective brief to an ineffective brief.

Delivering the Brief.

Most briefs will be fairly consistent in approach. From time to time you may have a brief that is either sensitive or will shock the team by its content. Where this is the case it is good practice to involve the shop steward before the brief, so that they feel valued by your trust. You may find that they help to deliver the content or support what you are trying to deliver.

Such pre-briefing will further deliver trust and respect as the shop steward has had a pre-warning of the content and will be able to remain calm during the delivery. We are not suggesting that you pre-brief on all communication, just the important ones where the shop steward will need to be seen to be taken into your confidence. Such an approach will be second nature at stage 3 of the MAP. By using this approach in stages 1 and 2 you will be assisting the development towards stage 3.

The content of the brief is important, and therefore should be of interest to all the team. However, you cannot rely on the content on its own to deliver interest. You ensure the message is interesting by investing in your method of delivery.

Good delivery will carry the message to the receiver and ensure it is understood. The basics in delivering an effective brief are your stance and your eye contact.
- You need to keep good eye contact with the group during your communication.
- This shows that you are confident in the topic.
- You can see who is listening and who is not paying attention.
- You need to keep looking at the total group as much as possible.
- You can look at your notes to give you a heads-up about the content, but then address the group with your content.
- This will look and sound more natural as it is coming from you.
- Your stance should make you look in command and confident.
- You should be upright and use open hand gestures to make your points.
- You can move around a little as it uses up any nervous energy.
- Try not to move too much as it will distract from the message.
- Keep open gestures, as when you fold your arms you look ill at ease and constrict your breathing. This in turn makes you feel uncomfortable and may lead to overheating of the body.
- A smile at the start of the brief will enhance your confidence - it will usually get a returned smile from the group.
- If you feel nervous, just remember this group need to hear your message as it helps them do their job. They want to hear what you have to say. Have a look at Appendix 1 to identify how to overcome nerves.

> I remember sitting in a briefing session with a technical manager who hated briefing her team. During the briefs they would read word for word what was in front of them. They never looked up or made eye contact with the team.
>
> By the end of the brief all but two of the team of ten had walked out and gone back to work. I talked to the team afterwards and they said work was better than listening to a dirge from someone who clearly does not care about the content or the team. I also spoke to the briefer who thought the team were so dedicated to their jobs that they went back to work rather than listen to the brief. They could not see that they were the issue

With any brief you need to be effective. One way to measure the effectiveness is the recall of the attendees of the main points. If the group can recall the key points they are more likely to enact them back at work. You can help the group remember the content in this way:

- Use simple language in a clear and controlled voice.
- Try to talk at your normal pace, as this is what the group are used to when talking to you at work.
- When you repeat key points, you help the memory of the receivers to retain the content.
- You can help this even more by using pauses at the end of key points or altering your tone of voice.
- The use of examples or relating to the group will enhance their memory.

- Give a summary of key points to remember at the end. This sends the group away with good clear actions to use back at work.
- When making your points ensure you are clear in your mind what you want the group to do.
- It can be useful to ask for questions after key points to ensure you clarify any uncertainty.

The more you practise briefing your team the more they will get used to the process. At first, they may struggle but with consistent messages they will start to understand how important it is to be well informed. The team will grow to like the experience as long as you maintain your commitment to the approach. You can use Appendix 1 to outline how to control your nerves if that affects your delivery.

Walking the Job

The best way to find out what is going on in your area is to walk the job regularly. In this way you see all of your team in their work space where they will feel more comfortable and will confide in you more willingly. The group will get used to the frequency and will grow to expect to see you during the working day. It is no excuse to say "My team can come and see me anytime, I have an open-door policy". This is a lazy excuse for not doing what good line managers do.

By walking the job consistently, you can get a feel for what is important to the team. You do not need to spend too long doing this, but you need to have a chat with each person. It is good practice to share your time out between the individuals in the team. If, say, you have a team of ten people, spend two minutes with nine of the team and five with the other member. By rotating the amount of time you spend with each person, you will ensure all ten team members get the five minute slot every ten visits.

Your visits should be seen by all those involved as useful. By focusing on the diagram below you can create a positive atmosphere with all those involved. The individuals will feel valued, involved and listened to. This will lead to the team generating extra effort.

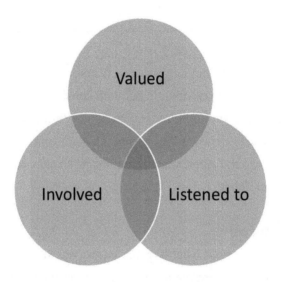

Don't forget that the shop stewards walk the job every day. They do this as they are part of the team and also get involvement from their members with their queries and comments. Therefore, they should have a good feel for the general sense of the team.

With this in mind you need to involve the shop steward in such sessions so that they are seen to be part of your team. I have always found it useful to have a regular (weekly) chat with the shop steward to discuss your findings. You can talk about the trends you are finding and see if it resonates with what the shop steward is finding. You will not identify individuals during such a chat as that is confidential, but you can talk in general. You are keeping each other up to date with the current feelings of the team. This is advantageous to both parties.

It does not matter what stage of the MAP you are operating, you need to be developing a relationship with the shop steward that will be seen as a trusted friend. This will take time to create but you need to start early in the relationship.

You can get a better rapport with the team member during a five minute chat as it allows time for a conversation to develop and will seem natural. To get the most out of the time this approach should be planned so that you allow the team member to talk about issues relevant to them. Also, you can use this time to reinforce key messages that help the organisation grow and will help the department be more effective.

When walking the job, ensure you have either a note book or pad. This is needed to record any requests or points to be addressed. If you keep such notes you are less likely to forget what a team member has asked for. There is nothing worse than putting the effort into being on the job but not following up on actions. This will appear to the team as a waste of time. They will soon stop giving their views.

By getting close to the team you will ensure any shop steward will not be able to surprise you with team views or requests. You are ensuring you are the person the team will ask if they have queries or requests. The shop steward will only take up your time with positive issues and most of these will be part of your walking the job. Most shop stewards will be pleased about this as they will not enjoy having to raise other people's problems. A good shop steward will refuse such queries and suggest the team member sees you directly. They will not get involved unless you have had a chance to address the issue.

If you find your shop steward raising other team members' concerns, you need to clarify that their role is not to take up individual cases unless they have been raised in the first instance by the individual with their line manager. This will ensure the correct route is followed in the future.

Never try to work through the shop steward when you should deal with the individual directly. This is the short route to building a power base for the shop steward and removing yourself from the day to day contact you need with your team. It may seem like a quick fix for a current problem but it will lead to greater problems in the future, as your team will believe this is the route they need to take and will bypass you in favour of the shop steward in the future.

Keep a log of the time spent with each person to ensure you do not miss a member out of the plan.								
LOG								
	Date							
Name								
A								
B								
C								
D								
E								
F								
G								

A good time for your first visit is either first thing in the morning or after the shift brief or daily update meeting. This allows time to talk and make an impact on the day's work.

> I well remember a colleague of mine called Mick who boasted about walking the job every morning. He was so proud of his achievement and would never sacrifice this task for anything else.
>
> I observed him doing this task one morning from a balcony on the site. He arrived and walked into the work area. He proceeded to wave at everyone as he passed and said good morning. He covered three rows of machines in about two minutes. He did not talk to anyone personally, he only walked past them in great haste.
>
> I went into his area and asked whether anyone had seen Mick today.
>
> The reply I got from the team was to ask who Mick was. I explained who he was and what he looked like. The team were unaware of his name as they called him 'The Phantom of the Opera' as he only appeared now and again and was always in a rush.
>
> It illustrates that the team do see what is going on and notice how we do our job.

Dealing with Queries

It is the line manager's role to deal with employees' queries as they arise. These may be identified by walking the job or any other normal contact event during the day or shift. The role also entails getting back to the employee as soon as is practical with a relevant answer. If you fail to get back with an answer, you might as well not have bothered pretending you will deal with the query in the first place.

You cannot say yes to every request, be it for holidays or a request to leave early. Your role is to ensure you give the person an answer with a clear rationale or a clear idea when you will supply an answer. This is reasonable as long as you give a decent timescale that represents the nature of the query.   You need to give yourself time to research an answer and ensure it is correct. If you have to consult other people in the organisation, ensure they are aware of the timescale you have set with the employee. When you have received an answer, pass it on directly to the employee in person. This retains your ownership of the raised issue. If an answer is expected to take longer than expected, this also needs to be passed on directly to the employee, with a reason for the delay.

When giving your reply always ensure the employee understands the response and the reasons for the response. This is most important where a request is refused, as the individual needs to be able to see that you have considered what they require but there is a good reason not to go ahead.

It is useful to keep a live record of all requests. This can act as a memory jogger. It can also act as a way to identify trends within your team. These issues can often be used as material for inclusion in a briefing session which will have relevance to the team.

By being effective with queries, you are showing your team that you care about what is important to them. You may not be able to say yes to all queries you receive but you can explain your reasons for the answers given. Always be positive about the answer. You know what you can and cannot support. The organisation's continuity must come first as that is what supports the jobs of your team and the rest of the employees.

I was involved with one company who were going through a major change brought on by a major decline in their market. It was agreed that all managers would spend more time with their team to ensure the workforce knew all about the proposed actions being taken. This seemed to be working well with most areas.

In one particular area the team were not convinced that the changes were needed. They were suspicious about the amount of time their manager was spending with them and seemed to believe the change was a con. When the group were asked why they did not believe the situation, they explained that they only see their manager when there is trouble, and yet again this has proved to be the case. The team were so tuned in to not seeing their manager that they tended to only believe what the loudest people in the group said. You need to be communicating regularly so that the team trust you and not someone else.

At times a shop steward will approach you with the person's query that has been refused. You need to ensure you are consistent and need to back your original decision if it is well considered. Unless new and relevant information is received you cannot alter your decision. If you are seen to change your mind too readily with the shop steward, you will have every refused query challenged. This will make your role uncomfortable. If new information assists a change of mind, ensure it is you and not the shop steward who takes the changing news back to the employee. You need to retain the flow of information to your team. This allows you to explain why your views have changed. A good move here is to return to the individual and ask them to explain the new information, which will allow you to be seen as listening to the individual and not be seen to be bowing to shop steward pressure.

Feedback

How often have you been surprised when someone says that they admire what you do, or how you handled a specific situation? I am sure, like most people, feedback like this is all too rare. When we get positive feedback, it makes us feel good and want to do even more. This is what we would all like from our team, so we need to develop methods and opportunities to make this happen.

If all of our teams felt motivated about their job in the organisation, our role would be so much easier. The need for a trade union would fade regarding negative issues and may focus on positive moves to sustain and maintain the organisation. This would appeal to most shop stewards as they tend to prefer making a positive difference as they will be at the top end of the MAP (stage 3).

The word 'feedback' can be seen as mainly negative due to past experiences we may have had at school or in other roles. It can be used to:
- Improve performance.
- Act as a motivator to make the required changes.
- Compliment on and consolidate the positive performance of an individual.
- The praise should be genuine and relevant.
- Recognise how best to maintain that performance.
- Enhance the performance of all concerned.

Feedback is not that easy to use if it does not happen effectively at the moment. It requires a skill and an ability to put time aside in order to give appropriate feedback. If you can do this effectively you will ultimately get the positive results you require, but you need to recognise that it will take time. It is worth the effort to have motivated staff.

There are two main sources of feedback - formal and informal. The formal feedback is by some form of agreed mechanism such as an appraisal. This will take place at set times of the year. The informal feedback is a regular and unpredicted event that occurs only when appropriate. The constant regarding the two types is that it takes place between the line manager and the employee.

Informal Feedback

This is by far the most effective type of feedback as it should happen at the time of the incident that required feedback. In this way the person is getting the feedback when they can clearly recall what has occurred. It is a great motivator for the individual as it is still clear in their memory.

Good managers notice the performance of their team members. By walking the job or just being in the work area one can observe what is going on with the individual's performance. Being alert to what the team are doing and how they interact will give plenty of opportunity for feedback. A good manager can see where someone has performed in excess of the norm or has failed to achieve their potential. Both of these instances are ideal for a feedback session with individuals.

The manager needs to ensure they use a private area to give constructive criticism to a team member. This avoids the individual being embarrassed by what others see and hear. It will ensure they concentrate on what needs to improve and how it will happen. Feedback in the form of praise can be delivered in front of others providing the individual is extrovert by nature. More introverted people will not appreciate the sharing of their praise in front of others.

A good way to offer feedback is the BOOST model. This focuses on positives and how to either maintain performance or make the necessary improvement.

Balance

Observed

Ownership

Solution

Timescale

Balance

Always start with a balance to the feedback. This involves talking about how good the person is in a particular area. This needs to be fact based and genuine. You need to use relevant and current examples that the person will know are genuine.

Observed

Talk about what you have just seen in the performance of the role. Be specific about the skill or behaviour and where it fits into what is required to be effective. Try not to be judgemental as it will take away from the focus.

Ownership

Try to get the person to agree with what you have observed and what needs to either improve or was good performance. It is easier to agree to good performance. However, without ownership the individual is unlikely to accept the feedback. Once feedback is owned you can make positive moves forward.

Solution

This is the section where the individual needs to develop their own approach to the issue and create a relevant and practical solution. You will at times feel frustrated by a lack of input here. The aim is to be persistent and not give your own solution. Individuals are more likely to change if they own their own solution.

Timescale

Give yourself time to consider what you are going to say and how it will be received by the individual. Try to be prompt with the feedback and don't delay for days, as the individual will forget what happened.

Example 1 - Improvement

Balance
You are one of my best operators I have in the team. I can trust you with any work on your machine as you work to the agreed standards and deliver all work on time.

Observed
I have noted that when you move to another machine the quality of your output drops by 10%.

Ownership
How do you see that?

Solution
So, what can we do about this situation?
Allow the person to talk and only discuss their solution.

Example 2 Praise

Balance
I like the way you handle the customers when they come to visit the site. You use their names and include them in the briefings as well as whatever is happening on site.

Observed
An hour ago, I observed you dealing with a difficult situation where a customer wanted a refund for a faulty product. You managed to persuade them to take another replacement product instead. That is just the sort of approach we need to take, as the customer was very happy and we have retained them using our products.

> **Ownership**
> How do you feel about that?
> Get a response
>
> **Solution**
> Can you see ways to do that more often? Listen to views and discuss.

If we have employees who are motivated to improve what they do and get good and regular feedback, we can develop an engaged approach. This takes away the need for any shop steward involvement in areas involving individual performance, as we will not need to discipline members of our team for poor performance. The team's performance levels or output will always be heading towards improvement.

There is no reason why you cannot offer feedback to your shop steward about how you view their performance. It is best to start this with a few positive issues so that they get used to the process. You can move on to more difficult issues later. If this is seen to work effectively, you can try to encourage the shop steward to offer you feedback. This will make your performance better and will enhance your relationship if you take the comments on board and make a positive difference. Such feedback will assist the process of moving through the stages and build a better relationship.

Formal Feedback.

Formal feedback is where the two parties i.e. manager and staff member review how they are working together to deliver the goals of the organisation. There will be different formats of appraisals for different organisations. The important thing is that the two parties must own the process and look upon the discussion as a positive intervention.

Too often I have seen organisations have a process for appraisals but it is not followed. This is usually because one or both parties do not understand the need for the process. The manager will say "I talk to the team every day, so they know how well they are doing". The employee will often say "The manager is not here enough to be able to judge me".

What this means is that both parties have 'lost the plot' with the formal feedback. This is not a memory session about who remembers the most. It is a review of the job performance and future needs. In general, most managers do not talk about performance or future needs on a regular basis, so it is no wonder that the team may lack the insight required to deliver a positive appraisal. Most employees are afraid of the process as they see it as a way to get negative feedback. They generally fear the worst from the process.

By making the appraisal a proper two - way process you can avoid this. Both parties need to:

- Know and understand the need for the process.
- Understand what both will get out of the time they spend together.
- Know how to prepare effectively for the event.

To do this we need managers who will:

- Show their own personal commitment to the process.
- Take time to explain the process and any changes that are different from the last event.
- Encourage the other party to prepare by outlining areas they intend to cover, well in advance of the meeting.

At the meeting the manager must:

- Stress that the appraisal is a two-way process.
- Allow the person to express their views.
- Take relevant notes of the key points.
- Show you are listening to the other person.

> - Summarise what has been said.
> - Where there are difficult areas they can agree what will happen in the future, rather than dwell on the past.
> - Commit to improve
> - Look at the support that is required.
> - Stress how you will help and review the improvements.
> - Give positive advice and praise.

Where you have an organisation that is driven to improve and has the support of the workforce, you will see less shop steward involvement in negative issues. They can spend their time on a positive approach.

In my experience, I have seen that where informal feedback and formal feedback are not working, you get more shop steward involvement in grievances and discipline. Most people do not want to spend time in those areas. You can overcome this by delivering good and effective regular feedback to the workforce.

It's How You Do It.

We have looked at the various tasks you should perform to be an effective manager. It is true that performing these tasks will help to generate a fully engaged workforce. What is equally important is how you perform these tasks.

I am sure we have all been in a situation where someone has performed a task but it is clear by their manner that it was done reluctantly. Such an approach will generally leave us feeling negative about the interface, even though the right thing was done. What is just as important as the task is the way it is performed. If you do not create a positive approach you will be wasting your valuable time performing the task as it will not have the positive effect on the situation you desire.

You need to create an impression that what you do is important to you as well as the organisation. In other words, what you are doing matters and will make a difference. This can be done by always delivering what you say and following up any items raised. Be fair in your dealings with your team.

More importantly is that you should behave in a manner that is positive, enthusiastic and genuine. You need to show that you believe that what you are doing is right.

You can create this impression by:

- Using open gestures
- Keeping good eye contact when communicating
- Showing you are listening by repeating back what you have heard or making notes
- Being consistent in your approach
- Using the first names of the team
- Getting to know something about the person away from work
- Taking an interest in the person
- Sharing your views openly
- Supporting the key messages
- Being fair and consistent

The last area of being fair and consistent is so important to your team. The team members need to feel that if they have dealings with you, the outcome will be consistent and fair. You therefore need to treat each person as an individual, but at the same time have no favourites. Each person should feel that you have considered their views before you make any relevant decisions.

This does not mean that you should agree to any requests. What it does mean is that you should consider all requests equally but fairly. If you are unable to agree to a request, the person should understand why you have said 'no'. They may not like your explanation of your decision but they need to have the reasons. In time a team will understand the boundaries of what you can and cannot do with regards to requests. This will be because you have acted in a consistent manner.

This part of the role is difficult but essential. Being consistent and fair will be appreciated by the team when they get to know you as a manager. Generally managers who say 'yes' to all requests will not be respected by their team. Usually the team take advantage of such people and this leads to a breakdown in team results. You want your team to respect you and deliver the key results. You are more likely to achieve this with a consistent and fair approach.

We have looked at what good managers should do to manage their workforce. Where they do this well they will get positive results and less involvement in negative interface with their shop stewards. They will spend more time with the shop steward in a positive environment. We need to look at this involvement with the shop steward as being mainly at stage 3 of the MAP. This is where both parties are getting the best out of the relationship.

By being a good and consistent manager, you may have to deal with more important business matters with the shop steward. This will help develop both of you as people and it will make your relationship stronger as you are dealing with less emotive issues, which can strain a relationship. By mainly looking at 'big picture' items you are both developing the organisation and its effectiveness for the good of the workforce. This can only strengthen job stability and enhance personal job satisfaction for both parties.

We are not trying to imply that good managers will avoid their shop stewards as they are doing a good job. We are saying that your involvement will be of a more positive nature and will relate to more business issues rather than what will be seen as day to day issues. By doing all of the above you will do what good managers should do - we all know that this does not happen with all managers. The time you spend doing these simple but important tasks will save you trying to play catch up when you require your team to be engaged.

Let us look at what you feel you need to do to be more effective with your team. If you look at Exercise My Improvements, you will see that there are areas of the job where you may need to improve. List the issues you need to work on and identify what you can do to address these in a positive manner.

My Improvements

	Issue	Actions	Timescale
Briefing			
Walk the Job			

Talk to the Team			
Feedback			

You now have a few items to concentrate upon. Make sure you take the time to deliver this action plan so that you get even better results in the future. Good Luck.

Key Points

1. You have to manage your team.
2. Keep the team updated on progress.
3. Walk the job regularly to keep in touch.
4. Offer regular feedback to all the team.
5. Review your approach to the team regularly.

Chapter 7:

Building a Positive Relationship With Your Shop Steward

In the previous chapter we looked at what good managers should be doing to get the best out of their team. A by-product of this is that your dealings with your shop steward are more likely to be about more positive issues. We now need to look at the important area of building effective relationships with our shop steward. If you are doing all of the tasks in the previous chapter, this relationship build should be fairly easy. It is recognised this will not always be the case. We need to look broadly at how such a relationship can be developed.

You need to try to develop a positive relationship with your shop steward as it will build on the positive environment you have created with the total team. We need to spend some time examining how we can achieve this situation as it will make your impact on the organisation more positive, as well as that of the shop steward.

You can look at the relationship by using the three circle approach. This demonstrates that you need to consider three inter-dependent circles to get the best out of the relationship. These are Personality, Skill and Common Goal.

Relationship Components

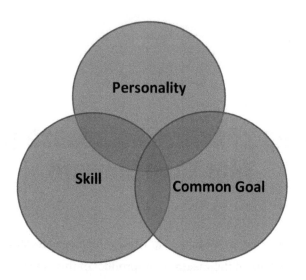

If you can consider how best to balance these three areas you can develop a successful relationship. The common goal will be developed over time but needs to have a business focus. The skills of both parties will develop over time. However, the personality of both parties needs to be a factor in the relationship. You will see later in the chapter how you can identify the shop steward's approach and be able to match it to yours to get the best results.

If we look at shop stewards, they will have different skill sets and behaviours, as will any person in your team. You need to recognise that you have to develop a positive relationship in order to build trust and respect between yourselves. You have to own the situation and make it your job to create the correct working relationship.

Most newly appointed shop stewards go through three main stages of their development. They will be learning about the role when first appointed and then will become trained to perform the role. Finally, they will act in a confident manner in their dealings with you and their members.

Stages of Development

	Confident
Unearned Confidence	Capable
	Learning

When a shop steward is newly appointed you need to meet with them as soon as possible. The meeting should be positive and focus on a discussion about how the role should be applied, and any help you can offer in settling into the role.

You should establish:
- Why they wanted the role
- What they hope to achieve
- What they know about the role
- What assistance/training they require
- How often they want to meet with you
- What skills they bring to the role

You need to explain:
- How you see the role
- What you expect from the shop steward
- How you would like to build the relationship
- Your experience of dealing with shop stewards
- What you will do to assist the person to succeed
- How you will review their training

This should be a pleasant meeting as you are both setting the scene for the future. You will be supporting the training of the union rep and can review their training as it unfolds. It is the perfect time to iron out any issues that can arise regarding the role or any outstanding procedural items.

You need to keep regular contact with the rep during this stage to ensure they are keeping to the areas of the agreement and are not attempting to get into other non-related areas by accident. You also need to ensure they are attending and getting value out of their training. You should meet the person as soon as possible after each training session. This will help you identify if they have gained the skills they will need to perform the new role.

A typical early problem you will face together is the rep who comes with an individual's issue you are unaware exists. The rep will take on the case thinking they will be seen positively by the workforce. You need at this early stage to be firm and insist the person comes to see you with the issue. You then have an opportunity to address it. All too often the person raising the issue knows it will not be successful, but they use this to test out the new shop steward.

If you allow the rep to act as a go-between, you will be stuck with that situation in the future. The positive relationships with your team will start to reduce as the shop steward will be seen as the go-to person, not you. This will undermine your status as the manager.

This is a problem you may face at any stage of the rep's development. Always be firm and take ownership of the problem. The new person may be just being helpful, but in the long run they will learn that it is not their role to champion individual issues.

If you adopt the right tone during this stage of the rep's development, you will be creating a good relationship on which to build in the future. You will be seen as trustworthy as you will have shown interest in the person and assisted them when necessary.

Capable

This will be the stage of development that will last the longest. Most trade union reps spend a long time consolidating the skills that were trained in the previous stage. They will be using these skills in the delivery of their new role. This will be fairly difficult at the start of the process but will ease as they gain experience.

The rep will get used to the role and will at first make some mistakes. These are only to be expected, as this will happen when anyone performs any new role. You should try where possible to minimise the effect of these errors. Where you can, it is advisable to coach the person to make them aware of what can happen if they take certain actions.

Whilst you cannot tell the person what to do, you can advise them of what they are doing and make them aware of the consequences. You can use the WIFI approach.

- **What If...**
- **Future Impact...**

By looking at what you intend to do you should also look at the future impact it may have on the situation. This is a good approach that will open the person's eyes to the consequences of their actions. By sharing this technique with the rep you will enable them to use it in the future when dealing with you as well as their members. It will aid a more thoughtful approach.

The more you protect the shop steward in the early days, the more you cement the trust and the relationship. This helps to keep their reputation intact and ensures their members are satisfied with the job they are doing.

> I remember a situation where a drayman (beer delivery driver) returned from holiday in America. They had seen a new approach to beer delivery on their travels. This new approach was positive and minimised the impact of lifting. They were keen to have the same vehicles with forklift trucks attached as they had seen in the States.
>
> The drayman clearly thought this would make life so much easier for himself and his work colleague. What he had forgotten is there is only one person making the delivery in the States. Therefore what he was proposing was the introduction of a new fleet of vehicles that would cost millions and a reduction of headcount by 50%.
>
> Such a move would seem fine on the face of it but would be unacceptable to the company because of the cost, and unacceptable to the workforce because of the lost jobs. As a new representative this person had let their emotions take over the situation, rather than look at the facts and use the **WIFI** approach. A simple chat saved the embarrassment of putting this forward formally.

I have always found that the WIFI approach helps when looking at any change type situation. It helps you to focus on what matters as well as making you consider any unforeseen knock-on effects which can catch you out later. It is best if both parties are familiar with this technique. Let's try and apply it to either a new situation you may face or one you have recently faced. Use Diagram 'the WiFi exercise' to record how you now see that situation.

WIFI EXERCISE

Issue_____

What If	
Future Impact	

As you can see, this gives a good indicator of what can happen if you consider the alternatives. It can prevent you from making hasty decisions you may regret later.

Confident

This is the stage you will want all of your reps to achieve. Unfortunately, most do not reach this stage as they have either come to the end of their tenure or have resigned after finding out that the job was more difficult than they thought.

It is during this stage that the relationship and trust will be high between both parties. They will have been involved in a lot of issues and come through them with mutually beneficial solutions and even a few conflicts, as it is not always smooth.

You will want to ensure you maintain this relationship and use it to take the organisation forward. The rep. will see the big picture but will be no pushover. They will be a person you can talk to in confidence without fear of the conversation becoming public.

I have been involved in many a situation where the shop steward has come to me or a colleague with information that is sensitive but helpful. On one occasion I was made aware by the shop steward of a group of employees who were conspiring to take products from site for sale to outsiders. This was theft and would damage our sales in the local area.

The shop steward wanted to remain out of the issue but believed it was their role to look after the business, as any theft would not only damage the business, it could endanger some of their members' jobs. This is an adult approach as it has a win-win outcome for the employees and the organisation.

You will see that the stages of development of the skills of the representative will closely follow the MAP. We have found that most representatives' development fits into the MAP as follows:

MAP

Stage 1 - Learning

Stage 2 - Capable

Stage 3 - Confident

There is another stage that not all representatives go through as it is exceptional by its nature. We name this stage 'Unearned Confidence', which tends to be stuck at stage 1 due to the nature of the conflict in the relationship. Let's look at this stage of development.

Unearned Confidence

This can be the worst type of representative to deal with as they believe they are good but have probably not earned their reputation in a positive way, or not earned one as of yet. They are far from good, except in their own mind.

You will be able to identify these people as after their first training session, and in some cases even before it, they believe they know everything. They are more likely to challenge what is going on in the department and will usually have little regard for the manager.

This type of rep. generally will not listen to you and will be constantly talking to their union about minor issues. They take this unearned confidence from the backup they get from their union. There is nothing wrong with taking advice from the union as it is part of the role, but even the union get fed up with such people after a short time. They may be useful to the union as they will follow what they are told and may try to address issues that are not relevant to the current agenda.

You will need to spend a lot of time trying to build a good relationship and trust. My experience has shown that this will mainly be time wasted, as such people are usually following their own agenda. Thankfully the people they represent will know this and generally don't respect them.

One way to prepare to tackle this behaviour is to have solid examples and facts about what has happened. You need to keep a log of events that shows what has happened on each occasion you meet. As a matter of course, I would keep a similar log for all your reps. It will show any disparity in their performance. The main reason for the log is to be able to show correct examples when necessary, as well as being able to summarise the main issues you face.

Log

Date	What Happened	Resolution	Date Completed

As you can see, such a log will enable you to recall issues from a time past your normal memory. Most people will only have a good memory that spans around one month, and after that we become vague. By keeping the log of issues and behaviour you will have a better recall of the main things that have happened.

If this behaviour continues you will need to do something about it to try and get back to where most reps will be. Only you can address the issues as it is you who is facing the person and their attempts to tackle what they see as unfair.

The best way to address this is to make sure the full-time officers of the trade union are aware of your concerns about the person and how they are behaving at work. This needs to be done in a non-aggressive way so that it is given a fair hearing. You will need to show concrete examples of how the person is behaving and contrast that with other reps. The union may help with the development of the person.

You also need to take steps yourself to address the issue of the behaviour. This needs to be in a non-threatening way that should be phrased as 'clearing the air to move forward'. By arranging a private discussion with the rep you can in a structured manner address your key concerns.

Use positive approach

> The meeting should cover the following areas:
> - How do you feel you are performing as a rep?
> - How do you see your role as a rep?
> - What are your intentions as a rep?
> - How do you view your role in the organisation?
> - Do you see yourself as an employee or a union rep?
> - How do you think you are viewed by the area you represent?
> - How do you think you are viewed by me?
> - What is your relationship with the trade union?
> - What is your view of the organisation?
> - Do you see your current behaviour as a rep as acceptable?
>
> You can then share your views:
> - How you see the person's performance as a rep.
> - How you see the person's relationship with the staff, other reps, the union and yourself. (Have relevant examples)
> - Explain what you feel needs to happen to bring about a change.
> - Express your concerns about their performance and where it will go next.
> - Discuss an action plan for improvement.

This type of discussion will not work on its own to change behaviour. You need to follow up their progress after the meeting and offer praise when it is due. You also need to tackle their performance when it is unacceptable - this needs to be done as soon as possible after any incident.

The person should always be clear that this will not go away. You must show determination that you will not let the standards drop or ignore issues.

It is good practice to keep the union officials aware of the actions you are taking as you are not satisfied with one of their representatives. Keep them up to date with any relevant developments so that if ever there is a major issue you have done your best to rectify the situation.

Never give up, as this is usually what the person wants. Giving in will only make your life worse as you will have even more frustration with the person.

Using the MAP to Develop Relationships.

Once your shop steward has been appointed you need to start the process of relationship building. You know that they will go through the three stages of personal development from the content above. You should also concentrate on the three stages of relationship building identified in the MAP.

You are trying to develop a positive working relationship that will lead to more of a partnership approach. This cannot be achieved overnight and will build gradually. You need to concentrate on each of the three stages and work effectively through these to establish a great working relationship. Let us look at each of these stages in turn.

Misalignment

This where either you are new to the shop steward or the shop steward is new to the role. You are starting from a position of having to get to know each other and how you both work. The first step is to get to meet the other person and introduce yourself. It is useful to explain what you expect from the other person. If the shop steward is new to the role you will need to establish what assistance they may need in the early stages of their new role.

It is important to be positive and open in your approach. You are looking for a problem-solving relationship, not one based on conflict. Your start should mirror that approach.

In your early dealings with the person you should continue to offer assistance. This will be especially needed when a first disciplinary hearing happens. Reps will feel vulnerable during their first exposure to this environment. You can build trust by explaining what will happen and explain the procedure in advance to assist with the confidence building.

Having regular informal chats about progress or just updating the rep will be useful early on in the relationship. Just as important is to support their training for the new role. By taking an interest you can still offer relevant assistance if necessary.

You will gradually build the confidence of the new rep and at the same time will be developing a trusting relationship.

Acknowledgement

You will normally achieve this stage after the person has been trained and has had the opportunity to practise their skills. They will start to feel confident in most situations they are asked to perform. By keeping regular contact, you are ensuring the relationship is positive. You can still offer help, but such help will be required less often as the skill level grows.

Together you will feel more comfortable and any meeting will seem natural. This does not mean that you will agree on all issues. You will have conflict from time to time and you will disagree on some issues. What you will also have is a high degree of trust and a developing respect for each other's skills and approach.

You will be able to more readily review the situations you have faced together and identify how this could improve. The maturity of the relationship will allow both parties to be critical without taking offence. Such discussions are valuable as it builds further respect and trust. The key element of success here is to take positive actions based on the discussions.

Partnership

The final stage of the relationship should be the target for all positive parties. This is where respect and trust have been built between both parties and they feel free to discuss items openly. The parties will respect confidences as this will have been tested and earned in the past.

The manager should see the rep as an asset who has a considered view that needs to be listened to before making key decisions. Both parties will have the ability to persuade and will use them when necessary.

The norm will be a stable and fairly predictable relationship. This does not mean that the rep is in the manager's pocket. What it means is that the two parties are experienced in dealing with each other and will be able to usually predict the other person's response to an issue. This shows a degree of predictability based on working together over a long period of time. We can do this with people we know well. We may not always be right, but we will have a 90% chance of being correct.

You develop this stage by being fair and open in your dealings. An honest person who takes time to explain their views will be seen as a good manager. This is not easy to achieve but you need to want to get there. Most of this will be attained by having regular contact with the rep and a consistent approach to issues that is based on sound forward thinking logic.

Inherited Representative

We do not always get the luxury of a new shop steward, as we may be promoted into a new role or join a new company. In both of these cases there is likely to be an existing representative who has developed a relationship with the previous manager.

I have seen many cases where the previous manager has described their shop steward in the worst terms possible and deemed a good relationship as a mere pipedream. These words will seem true to the previous manager as they are based on their experience.

I urge you to be open minded about what you will inherit. You may well have a difficult time, as the other person predicted; that is the worst case scenario. You may develop a great relationship as you are a different person and one who may operate in a different manner, so try your best to create a positive environment and build the trust and respect.

Sometimes you will find practices you either do not like or which are contrary to the agreement. Take your time to observe what is going on and develop a clear path to address what you encounter. Remember, the previous manager has allowed this to happen and there may be a good reason for it. Try to find this out before you act to correct the situation.

I remember a good colleague who moved into a new job in the North with a drinks company. She was appalled at the behaviour of the shop stewards who shouted and swore at managers in every meeting she attended. The managers seemed to think this was normal and had accepted it as such.

She developed a plan to address the behaviour and talked to the people involved first, to ensure the plan would work and was practical. Within a few months, normal type meetings were the accepted norm on the site and the loud swearing was a thing of the past. This only worked because she planned and involved others.

If you don't like what you find, consider what you want and develop a plan you can share with others. Once you enact the plan, make sure you keep to it to make sure the new actions happen. In most instances an open conversation is enough to sort a problem, as the other party is unaware of their impact. You can develop good relations if you try.

We may not all get to this point, but by trying to get there we will achieve the best we can, given our circumstances. Let us look at the current situation you face with your shop stewards. List which stage you feel you have achieved with the relationship. Then list how you will improve it further.

Current Relationship Situation

Relationships

Name	Current Position	Actions to Improve

Now you have identified the actions you will take, you need to ensure you follow these through. Look at this list from time to time to ensure you are making good progress. If progress is halted, revisit the work you have done and develop new actions.

Types of People

It is worth looking at the type of behaviour you may encounter in building relationships. This will help you build better relationships and also identify how to deal with different people in a way that will get the best from a situation. If we look at how people like information given to them, we can then develop our approach to them by giving our communication in a way that suits the receiver.

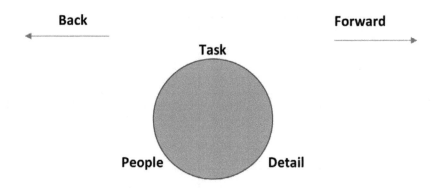

How people like to receive information

Most people like to get information in a way that suits their way of working. We can look at many variations on this approach, but we can make it easy by looking at the three main approaches shown in the diagram. This shows that people have three main ways to receive information that will keep them motivated to respond positively. These ways are:

- Task
- Detail
- People

If you can identify which is the main way people like to be communicated to, you can ensure you use the correct channel to make sure you are being effective. Of course we are all going to be a bit of each of these three types, hence the use of a circle to show we can easily adapt and alter our approach. Most people will have one preferred method that gets and maintains their interest. The trick for you is to identify this style and make your communication fit that approach. You are using the circle to adjust your style of delivery. It is unlikely that the person will be aware of the different approaches, so they will not consider changing their approach.

Let us look at each style in turn. Remember, no style is better than the other, it is just what the other person prefers when involved in communication.

Task

This is a style of communication that is direct and related to one main issue. It will be sharp and to the point. The receiver needs to know what you want and when it is required. If you try to add too much information, the person will get frustrated and lose interest.

You need to show that what you require will fit where the receiver's goals are aligned i.e. you are trying to achieve the same thing. The brief and concise approach will keep interest and will ensure the other person listens and may react positively.

Detail

This style requires the communicator to consider the depth of their issue. They need to offer a lot of relevant detail about not only what they want but also the detail of why, and the impact this will have on the current situation.

If you fail to offer the detail, you will get a series of questions that will be used to make the receiver comfortable with your idea. You may see this as a problem, the receiver may see this as necessary in order to be able to move forward. It is much better to anticipate these questions and build them into your communication. It will create a better impression and hence a better response.

People

This style requires you as the communicator to show you have considered the impact of your idea on the people in the organisation. Without the consideration for the people you will find you either get questions about the impact on people or resistance to your idea.

This may seem a natural approach to some of you, but you will be surprised how often this aspect is forgotten. It is often left up to the shop steward to raise such issues.

Responses

The responses you may get will be either forward-looking or backward-facing. Again, neither of these are better than the other. It is just the way the person tends to respond, and by identifying the typical response, you can be prepared.

The backward response is one where the person will have a series of objections or will say what they do not like. They will sound negative but what they are really saying is that they have some concerns about an issue. You should ask them to explain more or ask what they would prefer as a route forward. Either way you are starting to get a clear view of what has to be done.

The forward responder will generally say what they want in order to move forward. This may not be what you have offered but it will take you towards the objective. You need to ask the person for more details about how their views will help achieve what you have proposed.

With both types of responder, you should consider how your idea will go down with them and try to predict the response. This will help you to deliver your view with confidence and also tackle their responses with confidence. Both responses are natural and neither is intended to prevent progress. They are responses that need to be taken further in order to extract the required level of detail.

Let us now look at the people you deal with and try to identify how they like to receive information and their response style. This is useful as it may help generate ideas to enhance the relationship or develop a new approach to a difficult situation. It is also worth looking at your preferred styles as this has a great impact on the situation.

Styles Evaluation

Name	Delivery Style	Response Style
Self		
1		

2		
3		
4		
5		
6		

Now you have looked at the people you deal with, consider implementing an approach that will offer positive benefits to the relationship. Consider what actions you can take to move forward on the MAP.

Never take a response as a negative action; if you do you will fail to make progress as you are allowing the other person's response to be the final word. Their response is no more than a part of the overall journey and, as such, you need to keep the conversation going to get to a mutually agreeable final position.

Building relationships is not easy. It requires effort on both parties to get the best results. Once you feel you have made progress, you face the difficult task of maintaining the relationship. This is not easy to achieve but it is essential. If you take the relationship for granted you are likely to lose the goodwill you have generated. Maintaining a relationship is an ongoing task and can easily be lost by taking it for granted.

Let us now look at some final actions we can take to enhance our relationship with the shop steward and move forward on the MAP. Keep in mind the communication styles and the stages of the development of the person. Record your findings in the Future Actions exercise.

Future Actions

Person	Action	When

Now you have created your action plan for each person, think about how they may react. Be prepared to alter your communication style to address any issues. You should now have an individual plan for each person with whom you want to create a positive working relationship. You should try to enact the actions as soon as possible to get the results you require

Key Points

1. Ensure you get to know your shop steward.
2. Help new appointees to settle into the role.
3. Tackle those shop stewards who are not working for the benefit of the team.
4. Use the MAP to develop the relationship.
5. Always keep at the building of the relationship.

Chapter 8:
Consultation Meetings and Process

The consultation process is one that can often be seen as a waste of time by some managers. Some see it as trivial and time-consuming. The problem is that if the managers see it that way, it will never be valued by the workforce and, more importantly, the shop stewards.

"You get the consultative process you deserve"

In the UK we are bound by the European Directive For Informing and Consulting Employees. Any organisation with over 50 employees has to offer the workforce the right to be consulted. The consultation covers the business's economic situation, employment issues and prospects and any substantial changes in working arrangements.

The directive informs us about how we should consult via guidelines. However, most organisations tend to develop their own approach that best fits the circumstances they face.

The consultation process should be designed to give a business benefit to the long-term success of the organisation. If it is not working effectively, it is not just the organisation that will lose out, it is the workforce as well. That is more a waste of resources than a waste of time. List below the typical areas that are regularly discussed.

Working Positively with Trade Unions

> What does your consultative committee discuss?
>
> -
> -
> -
> -
> -
> -
> -
> -
> -
> -

The areas for discussion are usually outlined in the constitution. If you are not sure what you can and cannot discuss, you should look at the agreed constitution. This will be available to all managers, shop stewards and employees, either on the organisation's intranet or in the Human Resources department.

Most consultative bodies will include the following on their agendas:
The Business Plan.

- How the organisation is performing against the business plan.
- How and what the competition is doing.
- New ideas to move the business forward.
- Proposed new ways or methods of working.
- Potential new equipment and its impact.
- Issues of quality, service or products.
- Health and Safety.
- Working conditions.
- Staffing difficulties and recruitment.

I am sure you will agree these are reasonable issues to share with your shop stewards. In return you will want ideas and suggestions to make the concept more practical and saleable to the workforce. You may even want a high level of confidentiality around some specific issue that may be commercially sensitive.

If you are not getting these areas in return, you must be experiencing difficulty with the consultation process. You need to identify the cause of the problem. The cause of this will vary by organisation. However, our experience has shown that it will normally be down to the lack of training of the representatives, or the committee is not seen as effective by most people involved.

The C/I Technique

Keeping an agenda lively and creating the correct level of involvement is essential to any successful committee. Too often you can get confusion about what is being consulted and what is merely information giving, in order to keep the total workforce up to date. This confusion can lead a consultative process into conflict as the parties involved are unclear about how to handle the various issues.

The most helpful technique I have been shown is the simple C/I approach. This is used to identify the purpose of agenda items. If an item is intended to keep the team up to date it will be an information item on the agenda and needs to be marked with an 'I'. If an item is for consultation you mark it with a C. This is done prior to the meeting so that all parties are clear in advance about what will be consulted. This aids the preparation of the trade union team.

With a stage 3 team this will work well as there is a maturity about their experience. A stage 1 team may find such an approach useful as it allows them to see in advance that not all issues are consulted. It can reduce conflict as the team will know that the information being shared is to keep them up to date rather than to debate.

I have been in some meetings where the agenda is clearly marked C and I, but the shop steward still wants to have a say on the information items. One such example was when an organisation was looking at a new product, and the shop steward believed the company should be looking at other new areas to develop their products. The chair stated that this was the advice of the professional but if the shop steward wanted to pursue this further they could deliver a paper at the next meeting outlining their ideas. Such an idea needed to be costed and have a marketing plan.

This can end the debate about the issue and also leaves the person a route forward if they wish to take it. Anyone can find fault or disagree with a course of action; it is more difficult to find a positive and viable alternative.

Another alternative is to invite the person with the concerns to go and meet the ideas generator in the business. They can then have a positive discussion which could yield a better result.

When you are involved with such committees, it is easy to think that what is going on in the meeting is the best you can get. This may be your view, it may not be how others see it. You need from time to time to review how you are working together. This is more important for teams that are at Stage 1 and 2 of the MAP. Such reviews will help them move towards and even achieve stage 3 if it is done effectively.

To help identify how strong your committee feel about the current arrangements, we have a questionnaire that will help identify possible causes of problems. It should be issued to all the committee and the results discussed in a facilitated event. This will allow all parties to discuss how they feel about the current situation.

Our Committee Questionnaire

Please answer the following questions as truthfully as you can. If you do not know the answer, just leave it blank.

1. Do all members know the type of issues we are supposed to discuss at our meetings?

2. Do all members have an opportunity to have their say on issues?

3. Do we all listen actively to everyone's views?

4. Does everyone attend all the meetings regularly?

5. Are our meetings effective?

6. Do we all get enough time off to prepare for the meetings?

7. What has the committee achieved in the last three months?

8. Is the committee effective?

9. What would make the committee more effective?

10. Would you recommend being a committee member to others in the organisation

This questionnaire will generate a lot of relevant debate. It will show how the committee feels about their role and how others behave towards them. If the session is facilitated correctly you should get a number of good actions to improve the process back at work. You need to record these and ensure they are acted upon quickly. It is useful to review these actions from time to time, say every six months, to ensure the problems do not reappear. If you want to operate at stage 3 of the MAP you will want to make the necessary changes.

However, if you do nothing about these agreed actions, you will be in a worse place than when you started. Only go down this review road if you are serious about consultation and intend to make the necessary improvements. Doing nothing will either keep you at stage 1 or move you back towards stage 1.

A successful committee needs three key aspects to ensure it is effective. These are firstly that the team know their roles and how they work. Secondly, there exists a positive atmosphere within the committee, and finally there is a clear focus to the committee and the meetings. This may seem obvious but all too often one or more of these areas is missing. This leads to the committee lacking effectiveness.

Successful Committees

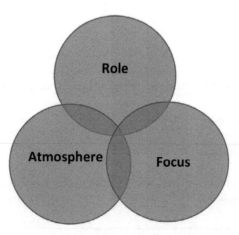

Let us look at these three areas to see what effect they will have on the shop steward involved in the consultative committee. By looking at this we can identify any areas we need to address to ensure we get the best out of the process and the individuals involved.

Role

This may seem obvious, but everyone involved in the consultative process needs to understand their role. Failure to do this will often lead to frustration on the part of those involved. It is best to outline the role before someone decides to stand as a representative. They will be aware of what they have let themselves in for. If this does not happen, we need to explain the role at the start of their tenure.

Some organisations do this in a training session where the process and roles are explained and discussed. Others use the chair to take new representatives to one side and explain the role. Either way needs to be two-way to aid the understanding and learning.

The role involves:
- Discussing issues with the staff in their area.
- Raising necessary issues at any pre-meeting.
- Attending pre-meetings.
- Actively listening to issues and input where necessary.
- Attending formal meetings and expressing the views of their area.
- Completing any necessary agreed actions.
- Feeding back meeting outputs to their area.
- Supporting staff in discipline and grievance cases.
- Advising staff correctly.
- Sharing relevant information with management and staff.
- Updating their skills regularly.

Too often, managers have problems with their shop steward concerning the consultative process. This is usually that the shop steward is going around their work area looking for issues to raise at the consultative committee. They therefore arrive at the meeting with local issues or issues outside the scope of the meeting. This usually happens with shop stewards that are at stage 1 of the MAP.

It is easy to refuse to include these items onto the agenda. This does not address the main issue - that the person does not understand their role. This is an indication that the shop steward needs to be briefed about what is expected from them and what they can and cannot bring to a meeting. If you fail to address this problem, it will not go away. It will get worse as the staff represented by the shop steward will feel the committee is not working. Also, the shop steward remains at stage 1 of the MAP and your relationship will mainly be based on minor conflicts.

If your shop steward knows their role they will not take up local issues, hence the staff expectations will not be raised. This will make the shop steward's role correctly focused and they will be seen to be effective by the staff. This will in turn grow the reputation of the consultative process and help take your relationship to stage 3 of the MAP. Fail to brief the person in advance and you are looking to heaven to intercede on your behalf, and this will not happen.

The meeting will have various roles to ensure it is effective. These will be:

- Chair
- Vice Chair
- Minute Taker
- Time keeper
- Participant

We need to ensure all roles work effectively if the meetings are to be effective. The chair needs to keep order and ensure everyone has an opportunity to take part. They need to stop anyone who dominates or keeps repeating themselves.

Finally, the chair needs to ensure they do not dominate the debate, as this will put others off contributing.

The vice chair will stand in for the chair if the chair wants to contribute on a specific topic. They will also summarise progress. The minute taker will note the key points that are being said and note any actions for each person.

keeper will ensure each item is allocated a time limit and will report on how time is used. This role is best circulated around the team at each meeting. Finally, the participant will have their say on issues and will listen actively to the debate.

The minute taker has a difficult role as it requires concentration and effort to stay focused on what is said. A method to assist this is to use Action Minutes. This records the key actions and allocates the task to a person, as well as stating a time of completion. This ensures everyone understands what is to be done at the end of the meeting. The diagram below can act as a template for the minutes.

Item	Action	Who	Timescale

From time to time you will need to review how these roles are operating so that the effectiveness of the meetings is consistent. This will assist you in developing the skills of the team. You can do this by open discussion or by observation of the team in action. The key is to identify what is working and what needs to improve. Take positive action to enhance the team, which will in turn develop the relationships within the process.

Focus

The focus of any consultative committee is what is stated in the constitution. It will usually be 'The development of the future growth or survival of the organisation'. This is a good intention at the start of the process. If it gets lost over time, it becomes very difficult to revive as the committee and individuals have probably generated a poor reputation. This can lead to being unable to attract good candidates for the committees as they do not want to gain a poor reputation.

If the focus is right, you will have an agenda that suits the growth of the organisation rather than one that has irrelevant and local items.

There is not one person who is responsible for the focus of the committee. It is the responsibility of all those who are involved. Too often the chair is blamed if the focus is missing. Whatever the case, it has to be everyone's responsibility as they can affect how the meeting is prepared and delivered.

The focus starts with developing the agenda. This needs to have a forward focus and look at items that cover the whole organisation. Any local items should be dealt with at a department level with the manager.

A typical agenda will be:
- Business Plan
- Business Plan update
- Financial situation
- How are our competitors performing

- What have we done since the last meeting (Action points)
- New agenda items
- Future changes
- Next meeting date and time

Such an agenda will keep the business focus, as any new items will be from across the organisation, not at a local level. All other items will be 'big picture' items so that those attending will be aware of the real picture of the organisation. This is an entrusted position where some items will be confidential. If items are shared inappropriately the chair will need to deal with the person who leaks the information. This often does not happen, leaks may continue and trust disappears. Finally, confidential information is no longer shared between parties and the consultation process is devalued.

You need to deal with all leaks to build the appropriate levels of trust. No matter who is the source of the leak, you need to ensure it stops.

Positive Atmosphere

When all members of the consultative committee have a clear focus on the process and understand their roles, you have a high chance of success. You just need to generate a positive atmosphere in the process and meetings. This sounds easy but like all things in life, it has complications.

This is built on an ongoing relationship that will be tested by outside factors as well as new entrants to the process. To be effective in this area you need to be thinking ahead as well as focusing on a daily basis.

We would all like to work in a positive atmosphere but realise this is not necessarily an everyday thing. There are a few aspects we need to consider, such as the physical working facilities and the working relationships and style.

Physical Working Facilities

We can often focus only on the meeting room we will use for our consultative meetings. This is important but it is not the whole picture.

The union team need access to ongoing facilities. These can be used for pre –meetings as well as sessions with staff. Not all organisations can afford extra rooms for this use. Where this is not possible, I have seen good managers give up their office to act as a hot desk for the shop steward when required. This helps show commitment but allows the manager to keep control of time off for union duties.

Any offered facilities need to be comfortable. That includes room temperature as well as lighting and adequate space. If such a space does not exist, you need to be demonstrating that you are trying to get the best that is available. You cannot do more than that.

The consultative meetings need to be in a well-lit and comfortable room. Again, it should be the best you can offer. It shows how importantly the meeting is considered by management.

Working Relationships Using the MAP

This is the real key to the success of the consultative process. All parties need to get to know each other and how they work. This is useful as a degree of comfort will be generated by people knowing each other.

This will usually be done in the form of a joint training session. When the individuals introduce themselves, they should be encouraged to talk about areas such as family and hobbies as well as work. You will always find people have more in common than they thought when a good introduction is delivered.

Managers can encourage this by going first or by interviewing each other against an agreed criteria, that covers work and social life. The more you know about your shop steward the better a relationship you can develop.

Respect and trust are two areas that will develop over time. You would like them to be present from the start, but life is not like that. People will trust you when you regularly deliver what you promise. You need to keep confidences and act proactively. Respect is earned over a period of time. This will relate to tackling difficult issues in a fair way and being consistent in your approach to issues.

Where you feel you cannot trust a shop steward, you need to talk to them about it and explain why you feel that way. By having an open conversation you are not only getting a new insight into their views but developing respect as you have tackled a difficult area.

I have worked with one team that was totally frustrated by the consultative process. The chair of the shop stewards was dominant and rude to both their own team and the managers. This led to conflict and a high turnover of reps. Most people would rather be somewhere else than the consultative meeting, due to the nature of the conflict.

The total team did a review workshop of how they related to each other. The shop steward's chair was shocked that his team believed he was doing a bad job and was creating a poor atmosphere. Their view was that they had to cause conflict because they were right in most things they did and management would walk over them if they were too agreeable.

This person just could not or would not change. Eventually they left the committee. Now this new committee has a great relationship and is making great strides forward in a way not seen before. Even the previous chair is astonished at the progress made.

By clearing the air and having an open debate you can make progress if you listen to each other and then act on what is agreed. It is useful to have such review meetings every few years. I have found that the most successful consultative committees regularly review progress and look to be even better in the future.

As a team you should encourage the concept of continuous improvement as a way of working together. It is the only way to move from stage 1 to stage 3 and develop a great relationship. By having such a relationship, you will find that shop stewards will remain in office longer, so you do not have to be constantly building new relationships.

You can use the MAP to determine at what stage your relationships currently lie. This will show you what you need to do as a total team to develop effective working within the consultative process.

If you are at the start of the consultation process you will be at the Misalignment stage. You are likely to have great expectations of the process but will have had little time to have developed effective relationships. By being open and honest as a team you will grow together. The more success you have with the relevant issues, the faster you will progress to the next level. You should expect some setbacks and conflict as the process is new. Do not hide from these issues as they have to be faced and completed.

By knowing these will occur, it will be seen by the team as part of their development rather than a setback. Time should be spent looking at how to improve as a team and how to use the various skills of the team. When you consider these points you will start to identify actions to use at future meetings to develop even further.

When you develop to the Acknowledgement stage, there will be a recognition of progress within the team. They will be more self-aware and more likely to offer their views in a professional manner. The team may not be fully developed, but there will be fewer setbacks and a major reduction in conflict as the individuals will see that the process works and more compromises lead to a better relationship.

This stage can still develop feelings of discomfort as there will be some challenges by individuals. The team need to identify that this is natural and will lessen as the group develops and uses its skills to tackle issues.

The final stage all good teams want to achieve is the Partnership stage. It is here that all team members will have a feeling of being valued for what they bring to the discussions. The inputs will be more relevant and structured. All the key issues will be more likely to be forward focused on the big picture of the organisation.

This stage will have a joint problem-solving approach that has all members seeing issues clearly but not necessarily the same way. Good persuasion skills will be used to help everyone arrive at a consensus decision.

No Agreement.

There will be times when you cannot move forward or it is too early to make a decision. This is not an unusual situation and has to have a solution.

At times you will agree a timescale for the decision or when the debate will take place. This at least offers hope of a solution.

There are other times when you 'kick the topic into the long grass'. This means both parties accept that there is no way forward at this point in time and further discussion is pointless. Sometimes the rep just wants to show their members that they have raised the point with the management team.

You will have built a relationship at each stage of the MAP. The relationship will be the best you can achieve given the circumstances of the committee's development. It will, in the main, feel comfortable as there will be a level of respect at each stage. The level of trust will grow as the committee works together and has a history of success together. The final stage will be seen as a good outcome where all members will enjoy the consultative process as it gives positive results for all concerned.

One problem all consultative committees face is the need to regularly have new faces. This happens when individuals resign, move on or are not selected by the area they represent. The committee is likely to have to regularly induct new people into the process.

New people can be good for the process as they will bring new ideas and a different level of enthusiasm. It is essential that the new members are up-skilled and inducted into the ways the committee works as soon as possible.

The committee is likely to move backwards regarding their total relationships as the new people are absorbed. The new people will need time to settle into the role and the process of the consultation. What has worked before may now be challenged. This is natural and should be expected by the established members of the committee. It is by being patient and encouraging that you will be able to get the new members up to the level previously enjoyed by all the members.

It is important to keep building the relationship on the consultative committee. You should never take the relationship for granted as it is a dynamic function of the members. You need to review your processes as well as how the group work together. The MAP can guide you through this area and offer practical ways to improve.

Let us look at where your consultative team operate. We can use the next exercise to record our findings. Look at what you do well as a team and then identify what could improve. Finally consider how you can make this happen.

Our Consultative Committee

What We Do Well	What Needs to Improve	Actions to Improve

You will need to identify and share your actions with the rest of the team. Think carefully about how to sell your ideas and look at the benefits for the committee. Finally, you need to look at when you should share the ideas. I am sure your ideas will make a positive difference to future meetings.

Key Points

1. Ensure all attendees understand their role.
2. Only accept agenda items that relate to the committee.
3. Create a positive atmosphere.
4. Get the physical environment as good as you can get.
5. Try to get consensus via a joint problem-solving approach.

Chapter 9:

The Negotiating Process (Terms and Conditions and Pay)

When talking to the average person in the street, they would believe that negotiating is the main activity of engagement between trade unions and employers. This is due to the publicity that is given to either a public dispute or the resolution of disputes on pay talks, as seen on the television, radio or newspapers.

In reality, we tend to negotiate on changes to working practices and pay no more than once per year. In fact, such negotiations are becoming even more rare with the prevalence of longer term pay deals and set pay limits, such as in the public sector. However, with the need to make business more effective, there are more opportunities to negotiate about issues that will make the organisation stronger and jobs more secure in the long term.

Most people who are new to working with trade unions feel that they will be seen by the shop stewards as inexperienced when dealing with negotiations. The same may be true in reverse when dealing with new shop stewards. Both parties may see the other party at stage 1 of the MAP.

In reality, we all have more experience than we give ourselves credit for with the negotiating process. We have been negotiating with our parents, partners and outside organisations all our lives. When buying a car, or deciding where and when to go on holiday, these are all part of our negotiating experience. What we may not have is a practical process to follow, but we are used to looking and considering the other person's perspective on the issue. Without a clear process it is difficult to replicate the negotiations and also have a process for reading the other party's approach.

Let us now look at a tried and tested method of delivering a successful negotiation. It is called POETS. This is an easy to use approach and can be used to monitor the progress you are making as well as analyse the other party's position and identify how best to make relevant progress. This will give you the skills and knowledge to negotiate better deals that will be acceptable to both parties. The POETS approach is like a road map that you can follow to gain a positive win-win outcome.

The POETS Approach

> **PREPARE**
> **OPEN**
> **EXCHANGE**
> **TRADE**
> **SETTLE**

We will look at all five elements of POETS and determine how best to use these to gain positive results when we negotiate with trade unions or other parties. We will also look at the best ways to get a positive outcome to a negotiation where both parties will feel satisfied with the end result. This tends to lead to long-term satisfaction and better and more trusted relationships.

If both parties are new to negotiations, it could be useful to share the process you intend to use. This will show you are trying to build a good relationship and are looking for a win/win approach. Teams that are at stage 1 of the MAP can progress forward if they share more in the early stages, as this will help build the trust and mutual respect.

It may be useful to look at the experience of our team and the shop stewards with regard to negotiations. This will help us identify where both parties need to put their efforts. Use the diagram to outline your views.

We now have an idea of each other's experience. It may be useful to discuss these views prior to the negotiations to ensure such views are correct.

Name	Experience

What is a Negotiation?

We can use the term 'negotiate' rather too loosely where it may not apply. You may feel you are going to negotiate with someone about an issue but can find that they do not want to talk to you or are unable to move their position. This is not a negotiation as the other party was not prepared to talk or move their position.

An example of this can be when booking a room at a hotel. If the hotel has one room left and it is 10.00 am, they are unlikely to offer a discount. They will not negotiate as they will expect to get the full room rate some time during the day, either from you or another party. There is plenty of time to sell the last room, so they will not need to make such a decision so early in the day.

If the hotel has, say, 100 rooms empty and it is 8.00 pm, you may get a different reaction. They may negotiate, assuming the reception staff have been given the authority to negotiate. A sensible person will want to get some revenue for the available room or rooms, depending on the price being offered. The hotel will still want to make a profit on the transaction, so they will not give the room away.

"A negotiation is where two parties try to settle an issue to gain a mutually beneficial outcome when starting from diverse positions."

If one party has no mandate to negotiate, we cannot have a negotiation. There are times where the mutually beneficial outcome may be the best you could get in a very difficult situation. It may not give you what you had hoped to achieve, but it will work. If this is the best you could get and it is mutually agreed, it is a negotiation.

Style of Negotiations

The style and approach to negotiations has an impact on the result. The news programmes give an impression of an adversarial approach to negotiations.

This is due to the language used after a negotiation and the possibility of strikes. It appears that the parties involved are fighting each other.

If this is the case, the outcome will take a long time to arrive as each party will be reluctant to move in order to save face. One or both parties will also feel aggrieved at the outcome and will try at a later stage to settle the issue. Such behaviour leads to long-term problems as trust and respect are lost. This can lead to poor employee relations as the atmosphere will ultimately turn toxic.

Quite often with national issues that are seen on television news programmes, you will see very aggressive language being used to describe the negotiations. This is usually for public consumption and the members. In reality the negotiations are often positive and non-aggressive, due to those who are involved being professional negotiators. This will surprise some people, but most people who have been involved in these situations will recognise that this is the norm.

The non-adversarial approach has greater benefits to all involved parties. However, it requires both parties to agree to the approach. You need to look at issues as mutual problems that need a joint solution. This has been the approach most modern forward-thinking organisations have taken with pay negotiations since the more difficult days of the 70's and early 80's.

By being non-adversarial you are more likely to create better and more creative outcomes that are respected by both parties. Such outcomes will be more accepted by the workforce. This leads to better ongoing relationships in other areas of employee relations.

If you think short term, you are unlikely to be bothered about the impact a deal will have on the other person or the people they represent. Once the other party identifies that you don't care, the relationship will become adversarial. You will compete with each other for a deal that will possibly only give short-term benefits.

An example could be where a trade union tries and succeeds in getting a large pay increase the company cannot afford, say 10%, when the norm for the industry is 2%. This may look like a good deal, but in the long term it could endanger further investment in the site and lead to job losses. We may say this is the employer's fault for giving the increase, but it is the fault of both parties for not looking long term. The employer has bought peace but has created a longer term problem for the security and success of the site.

Where your focus is on long-term relations, you look for deals both parties are happy with that ensure prosperity for the long term. Both parties will feel that the settlement is the best available deal at that time and will know that any failure to agree will lead to problems at a later date.

Let us now look at how the POETS process works. You will see that it is in five stages and each needs to be followed in the correct order. When one party tries to go too fast or miss a step, it always leads to confusion and a delay in progress.

Preparation

The key to any successful negotiation has to be the preparation. Without this step, everything that follows will lead to failure or is left to luck. I am sure you would not like to rely on luck for the outcome of an important negotiation.

The main areas of preparation you will need to focus on involve looking at your own position and that of the other party. This may seem obvious, but too many people just look at their own situation and fail to consider the other party to the negotiations. By looking at both parties you can estimate if there is an opportunity to gain agreement and identify issues that may prevent the agreement being achie

As a young HR Manager I recall a set of negotiations at a paper plant in Cumbria. I had been entrusted to research and deliver changes to the shift system for the Engineers. I had to deal with the senior shop steward for the site, who was a formidable man and carried a lot of sway on site.

After the research, I had discovered a great way to change the shift arrangements that would lead to little disruption if implemented, and no pay loss for those involved. It seemed perfect to me. It was so logical I was impressed with my research.

I decided to commence the negotiations and expected a quick and positive resolution. When I met the senior shop steward, I outlined my plan and how it would work. He duly took notes and listened intently.

Once finished, I asked for his views, to which he replied – You're not on, Marrar (local term for mate or pal)

I was crestfallen, and left the meeting not knowing where to go. When briefing my boss, he asked two great questions.

1. What reactions were you planning to get?
2. Why did he not like the shift plan?

The answer I gave taught me a great lesson. I had not considered a rejection of such a great plan and probably did not think at all about the other party's position before the meeting. Worse still, I did not ask him what he liked and disliked about the shift plan. So, I did not know how to address the rejection.

Great lessons, pity I did not think more during the preparation stage.

Looking at your own case first is a good starting point. You need to gain a budget for the negotiations. This involves the Finance team as well as the Head of Business. You need these people to offer what they believe is necessary to gain a deal.

The Finance people will also help you with a lot of the preparation. Never forget to involve these people as they are one of your most valuable assets. They will know how to cost a deal and give a breakdown of the costs of individual items.

It is advisable before talking to these people to have an idea about what you think will be a reasonable deal. The Finance and Head of Business are bound to ask what you think you will need to get a positive settlement. Not to have an educated idea will make you look unprofessional.

You will need to look at the following typical areas:

- Rate of Inflation RPI or CPI and the trends over the period of the deal.
- Current payment deals with competitors, local companies and national organisations.
- Review the benefits package with similar and local organisations.
- Identify the strengths and problem areas with your pay structure.
- Identify the issues you want to raise and change within the pay structure.
- Current market trends in your sector.
- Current financial situation of the organisation.
- What you believe are the expectations of the workforce.
- List the variables of the payment package and benefits of the workforce and identify what is valuable to the workforce and what is least valued.
- What are the concerns and inhibitions of the trade union?
- What are the national and local issues being pursued by the trade union?

- How will you overcome the inhibitions of the trade union?

When you discuss the company situation with the Head of Business you need to establish some clear guidelines. You need to know what the final agreed company position is and whether it will change with pressure. If it will not be changed due to trade union pressure, you need that reassurance. You need to determine how far the company will go to get a settlement.

There is nothing worse than negotiating, knowing that your boss will collapse if a deal is not agreed and add more money to the deal. This does not generate trust and gives off the wrong signals for any future negotiations. I have seen this many times where the Head of Business is the fall back, and always gives a little more. Thus, the trade union negotiators always know to refuse your best deal as they know a failure to agree gets a further increas

> I recall a situation a friend of mine faced when new to a transport company. The norm in the negotiations was for the trade union to vote on the final offer and the offer was always rejected and a threat of strike was imposed. The reason for this was on every occasion a rejection was made, the company always increased their offer to buy peace and avoid a strike.
>
> It was agreed that the cycle had to be broken and that no increased offer would be made: in fact, the offer was to be reduced by the cost to the company of the strike, if it happened. This was stressful for the CEO, who had always bought peace.
>
> The final offer was rejected by the vote and a strike was threatened. The management team explained that any cost of the strike would be taken from the final offer. After a one-day strike, the union were very surprised that the offer was not increased and furthermore it was reduced by 0.25%. A further one-day strike was delivered. On the return from the strike, the offer was reduced again by 0.25%. It was only after three one-day strikes that the union agreed the pay deal, which was 0.75% below the final offer.

> The reason for the strikes was that the union believed the mere threat would yield an increase. Once the management kept to their word about the reductions, the union started to believe that the final position really was the final position. It takes time for a new approach to be accepted. Future negotiations were better, as more understanding existed about how truthful the final position actually was.
>
> If you want to try a similar approach, ensure your CEO fully understands the difficulty the approach involves. It will never be easy to change built-in beliefs which are based around hard facts.

Each item of the pay deal needs to be fully costed. So, if you are talking about a change in the number of holidays, you know the total cost and how it will impact on the total amount available to get a settlement. This is real preparation that takes time and effort. It also ensures you do not concede an item that will cost more than you can afford.

You now need to start developing your position for the negotiations. You have to establish your starting point, which should always be realistic. This will encourage the other party to be positive. If the opening position is unrealistic you will get an equally unrealistic response that will not set the positive tone you desire. Your opening position is like the sticker on the windscreen in a car showroom. It needs to be realistic enough for a person to retain interest. If the price is far too high, the person will look elsewhere.

You also need to establish the furthest you can go in order to make a successful settlement. The budget will usually identify your furthest point but you need to look at how you want to spread that budget and ascertain the priorities that best suit the business. Consider how the other party will react to such a position. This may help you retain a realistic approach.

Any negotiations should consider three key areas of the final position. You need to consider if the deal is:

1. Fair
2. Affordable
3. Sustainable

If the deal is seen as unfair it may have little chance of success. If it is unsustainable the organisation cannot go forward and prosper as it will bring some problem areas. Finally it must be affordable. If the business cannot afford the deal, you will undermine the future of the business. In such a situation you are looking at a short-term fix that will probably cost jobs later. No one wants to willingly go into that situation.

You need to ensure that there is sufficient space for movement between the Opening and Furthest points. This will allow you to open in a realistic manner and ensures any movement is small but significant.

We call this the OMF. That is your Opening Position, Mid-Point and Furthest Position. This can be seen in the diagram. You also need to estimate the other party's OMF. In this way you can establish if you will get an overlap on the process and hence a settlement.

	OMF			Note of potential difficulties
	Opening	Mid-Point	Furthest	
Company				
Trade Union				

Let's look at our OMF for the current negotiations described above.

	OMF			Note of potential difficulties
	Opening	Mid-Point	Furthest	
Company	2%	4.5%	7%	
Trade Union	10%	7.5%	5%	

As you can see from the diagram, there is an overlap - therefore an agreement is possible. The area of overlap is the bargaining arena. As long as you settle in this area you will get a settlement that is acceptable to both parties. Your own best deal is the one that is closest to your opening position.

If there is no overlap you need to look at what is stopping the process. By identifying these areas or difficulties you can look at what can be done to overcome them if that is possible. You can identify areas that need to be explored and develop questions to clarify the information required. You need to be proactive in developing the way forward.

You now need to prepare for the negotiations. You have a clear brief from the Head of Business that allows you to deliver a settlement at a certain budget. You now need to select your team and develop an opening position script.

The team you have should include a person from Finance. They may not be one of the team who faces the trade union, but they need to be dedicated to costing any proposals. This person needs to work on potential scenarios and look at all the variables that are available and cost each one of the options.

The team need to be given roles for the negotiation. The main roles will usually be:

- Talker
- Scribe
- Observer
- Supporter

Scribe

The scribe is needed to record what is said and any nuance in the language or body language. They do not need to have a verbatim account, but merely a clear overview of what is said by whom. Such a person needs to be able to concentrate for long periods of time and not get involved in the discussion.

The notes need to separate what was said by both parties. It is useful to use a sheet that is separated into two halves. One side shows what your team said and the other side shows what the response was from the other party. This makes feedback easier in the recess. Putting a time of start and end of a session will help to demonstrate what is going on. Next is a typical scribe's sheet.

Get the facts

What we said	Trade Union
10.30 Start (J). We want to get an agreement by the end of the week. Q. (J) What do you need to share? Q. Is there any way we can help? That's fine by us. Let's say 30 mins. **9.42** Recess.	(P) That may be difficult as there is a lot to discuss and we need to talk to our full-time officer about the key points of the agreement. A. (P)The rate of basic increase and the change in benefits for all our members. We also need to check some of the wording of the agreement to ensure it is legal. It will not take long but the FTO is not available until next week. A. Let's recess to evaluate that. (Very nervous hands) That is good for us.

You can use the Q for Questions and A for answers, as shorthand, to show what is happening. You can include the note for who said what by putting their initials in brackets before any script. You can also note any body language or intonations that were relevant. These can be in brackets at the end of the script or next to the area where it was relevant.

Observer

The Observer has the role of looking at the other team and trying to ascertain any significant responses in body language. They need to record what they have seen against what was said at the time. This person needs to be able to observe more than one person at a time and keep a focus on the process they are observing. They should not fall into the trap of watching their own speaker deliver their views. Instead, they must look at the trade union team. Below is a useful document for any Observer.

What was said?	What did you observe?

Talker

The Talker is the person who delivers the company message. They have to prepare the opening and all other responses to the other party. They will be the focal point of the discussion. No one should speak without the Talker's permission as their input is unplanned and may stray from the points being made. The talker is the chair-like role in the team.

The talker will share the work they have done on each planned input. This will be in the form of a dummy run of the talk to the rest of the group. The group will be able to affect the input and add value. However, you need to guard against too much 'word-smithing' as it will prevent the Talker from being themselves. They need to use words which they will typically use at work. This will make the flow more natural and easier for the other party to understand.

Supporter

The Supporter will assist the speaker during the face-to-face sessions. They may be used to feed in ideas or summarise the key points before a recess. Therefore, they need to be keeping a set of summary-type notes during the session. They should also be the last person to leave the room in order to ensure nothing has been left behind.

Any role can call for a recess if they feel it is necessary. The rule is that if a recess is called, you all go. The recess caller will have a reason to call a recess and this needs to be respected by the total team. The speaker may at times feel they should continue to talk and keep a dialogue going. This may lead to deeper problems if someone has called a recess because they have seen a major problem with what is being said, or with the direction of the negotiations.

Opening Talk - Preparation

The talker will need to prepare the opening talk. This will outline the opening position of the company. It will show what the current thinking is and offer relevant reasons why this should be adopted. It may have some visuals if necessary.

The talker needs to perform at least two dummy runs of the opening with the team. This gets the team used to the content and allows them to influence the input. It also boosts the talker's confidence before the negotiations. Time should be spent developing ideas about the type of questions that can be raised by the other party. This gives time to develop answers or add to the opening to make it even more focused.

The team will at this stage be given specific instructions about what to look for as observers or scribes at different parts of the opening. Thus, the team are being prepared to carry out their roles effectively in the opening stage.

It is not unusual to have a copy of the opening script available for the other party. This needs to be proof read before using it to ensure it is clear and error free.

Recess Manager

During any negotiations there will be time outs or recesses in order to review progress and develop a way forward. These need to be managed effectively and you will need a person who will manage the recess. This is a key role as it will keep the team focused. However, it is a difficult role as keeping order can be tricky when a team gets excited about either progress or the lack of progress.

The recess manager needs to have a calm, controlling approach and manner as well as have a clear structure to the recess. They need to look at what has happened in the previous round of talks and then look at what needs to be done to move the process forward. The talker is not the best person for this role. They will be highly involved in the negotiations and need time to refresh themselves prior to the next face-to-face session.

The recess manager will need to involve the total team in an orderly manner, one at a time, in a review of the last negotiation session. The scribe can recall what was said, followed by the observer's comments. They need to relate to the OMF positions. We need to see how close we were to the other party's OMF and what still needs to be established. Focus needs to be on the company's OMF and what reaction was recorded.

Time should be spent looking at what stage each party is at on the POETS process. Once this is established you need to look at how to establish new information or what is needed to move forward to the next stage.

Tracking the progress of a negotiation can at times be difficult. You are looking at the stages of the negotiation (POETS) and your OMF. This is very useful. One can often lose sight of what you have proposed and what the other party has proposed. This can lead to confusion and frustration in the team as they go back over old notes.

This can be avoided by using a simple approach to monitoring each move that is made. You can develop on a flipchart a simple tracker of each movement. This needs to show the variables discussed and the offers made. In this way you can see progress and identify areas that appear to be difficult to remove. It will ensure everyone in the team is able to see the current position, providing it is added during the recess by the team. An example is shown below.

Variables	Offer / Response							
	Mgt	Union	Mgt	Union	Mgt	Union	Mgt	Union
Basic Pay								
Overtime								
Holidays								
Pension								
Hours of Work								
Canteen Subsidy								

Safety Wear							
Staff Discounts							

By marking offer 1 as the company, you can mark offer 2 as the trade union response. In this way you can see at a glance who has offered what and the response of the other party.

Finally, the talker needs to develop the next input or set of questions for the other party. These can be shared with the team in a dummy run format as before. You also need to identify any specific issues or responses to look out for during the next face-to-face session. All of the individuals in your team will know where their role needs to focus in the next meeting.

You need to spend time identifying the best person for each role. This is not easy as you need to look at each person's preference against their ability to perform a role. This is a time to be calculated about who does what. You need to be firm about the skills individuals bring to the team and their abilities to help deliver a positive result. Try not to compromise by keeping someone happy who will do a poor job in the role they would prefer to do.

Look at who is the best person to perform each of the roles you require and develop a back-up person in case of illness.

Who is in my Team?

Role	Designated Person	Back Up
Talker		
Scribe		

Observer		
Supporter		
Recess Manager		

The team are selected and should be prepared and ready for the next phase of the negotiations. We need now to look at the face-to-face aspects of the process.

Opening.

This is the most important of the face-to-face phases of negotiations. You get to set the tone of the process and establish how the negotiations will proceed. Often if this phase is delivered in an inappropriate manner, say an aggressive approach to a mild issue, the whole process will either break down or will take a lot longer to conclude. We have all heard someone say to the press – "We came to negotiate, and they did not, so we are available whenever they want, but they must be prepared to change their stance."

Whenever this happens it is a sign that the opening has gone wrong or the other party made it clear they did not want to negotiate. It is a bad start and makes life difficult thereafter.

Delivering the Opening

You must ensure the starting point is positive and welcoming. This means you have to not only say the right words but also back them up with positive body language, as well as setting a positive environment.

The environment for the negotiations is set by you. It needs to be clean, tidy and practical for the process in hand. That means you should have sufficient comfortable seats for all attendees and a recess room for the other party to use. This allows them to discuss your points in private. The meeting room needs to be large enough to fit everyone in and have plenty of space. Natural daylight is useful for creating the correct atmosphere for positive work.

Having fresh water during the meeting and tea/coffee on arrival also sets the positive tone. It shows the other party the appropriate level of respect and shows you are professional in your approach. Such an approach leads to less conflict.

You will usually be opening the meeting. It is useful to give an overview of the time allocated and the facilities you have developed e.g. tea, coffee and lunch arrangements. Making the other party aware of the recess room and where it is situated is a good idea. Finally, you should outline the process of the meeting e.g. who will open and what to expect from each other during the meeting.

If you are opening, be prepared to deliver your points slowly and deliberately. You will probably use a script to ensure you do not miss any points. To be seen to create an open and honest approach you need to keep some eye contact, especially when making key points. Give any praise to pre-work done by the other party and show you have considered anything they have raised regarding the issues. This shows that you have listened to their points and indicates that you will do this in the future.

A typical opening will cover the following four areas:
- The current situation in the organisation, sectors and any economic issues (Background to the negotiations)
- What you have done whilst preparing
- How you have prepared with sources of information
- What you propose to offer (opening offer)

You are delivering your best position which you would like the other party to accept. It must be realistic and show you have considered the other party's position as you know it. Your opening must explain why you are proposing the current position and why you feel it will offer an acceptable approach to both parties.

Never try to be aggressive or score points during this phase. It will not help your case and will give the other party reason to reject your views. If the other party tries to be aggressive or score points, don't rise to it. It is often just a show or is a way of getting rid of pent up emotions. Stay calm and don't react. It is best to use a quieter voice to respond as it makes the other party listen. If you raise your voice, you can start an argument, which will neither generate movement nor create a positive atmosphere.

Your team should be ensuring they capture any relevant responses (scribe) and reactions (observer). It is worth noting if the other party have been recording the key points you have made. If they have not, you will need to decide how best to get your points remembered in the next session. You can do this by either repeating key points regularly or by issuing notes.

The talker should have a confident voice and manner to demonstrate that they believe in what they are delivering. This creates confidence in the information being received. After the delivery it is useful to ask if there are any questions.

The talker can answer the questions if they feel confident to do so. It is better to note all questions first before answering, as you will get time to devise answers in the recess. This helps if you can answer some but not all questions. You will not appear to be confident if you only answer a few and then recess. By noting all the questions you can have a recess to develop reasonable answers to all the questions.

Before any recess it is useful to summarise the key points and questions you feel need to be addressed in the recess. You can say you will look at the questions raised and suggest the other party consider the points you have made. This ensures both parties have something to do during the recess.

An inexperienced negotiating trade union team may just wait for your responses and not consider your points. This leads to time being wasted and longer negotiations.

Receiving an Opening

You need to focus on what the other party is saying and how it is delivered. This is their best position and will show you what is important to them and their members. If they show confidence it will enhance their position. If there is a lack of confidence it could be because they have little faith in their position or they are inexperienced. You will need to look at this in the recess.

The talker will need to keep good eye contact with the other party to show that they are listening. Key points should be noted to show you are grasping what is said. The scribe and observer will need to engage their attention to the task in hand.

Always let the other person finish before you ask for any clarification or questions. This shows respect but also ensures you get the full story as it was planned by the other party. You need to understand why issues are important to the other party. If this detail is missing you need to ask relevant questions. Ensure your scribe is ready for this before asking the question. This ensures they get the question and the relevant answer.

Whilst this opening is being delivered you will be thinking about how this matches with your OMF plan for the trade union. In the recess you can look at this further with the help of your team. When you have all the information you require and have asked all relevant questions, you can recess to consider how to proceed.

I have been in negotiations where the other party has called a hasty recess. In their desire to exit the room quickly, they have left behind documents that relate to the negotiations. Such documents may or may not help you but you will read them out of curiosity. You will never know if it was a deliberate ploy to leave the documents behind. My experience shows it to be usually an error and in some cases the information has been to the detriment of the other party.

You can avoid the embarrassment of such an error by ensuring the last person to leave the room sweeps the table of all documents. Make sure your team remember to remove their own documents when leaving for a recess.

NB Negotiations are about momentum. The Opening is the start of the journey. However, there is no real movement until we get to the Trade stage.

Exchange

This phase is needed to ensure both parties have the information they need to move forward. It is likely to follow a recess, where both parties have fully considered the openings that have been delivered. It is inevitable that a lot of queries will be raised that need to be discussed before any movement can happen.

Both parties will have looked at their own OMF positions and that of the other party. They will now know the opening position of the other party and will be looking at how to get to the bargaining arena. A set of new questions will be developed by both parties. This will usually be to establish what is important and what is not important to the other party.

When the parties get back together there will be a need to have some order to what they do. It is usual for one party to respond to questions asked before the recess. These will be delivered and some discussion will occur. Be prepared by looking at potential questions you may face and developing appropriate answers.

The other party will then answer the questions they were asked. This will lead to further debate and discussion. This is all part of the exchanging of views and relevant information. It is normal to have another recess to consider where to go and how to develop that movement.

You can explore potential areas that are of interest in a tentative manner. Ask what the other party think about a specific idea. Let them know it is just an exploration of concepts. Whatever the reply, encourage the other party to say what is acceptable and unacceptable about the idea. Even more importantly, establish why they find it acceptable or not. In this way we are getting a shared understanding of the issues, without any real commitment.

During this phase you need to ensure you listen carefully and take good notes. An accurate summary of views will help the process of understanding each other's issues and inhibitions. This should be followed by a recess to consider what information was gained and what still needs to be established.

This may seem like a negative phase but it will help, as you will gain a full understanding of why views are held and the difficulties the other party faces. You cannot proceed forward without fully understanding the other party's position and issues. They also need to know the same about your situation. This will help you get a full picture with the OMF analysis in the recess.

The notes taken by the scribe are important at this stage as language may change. What started out as "Impossible" in the opening stage may now be "Difficult". Not only that; you should now know why it is difficult. As the negotiations proceed, we can learn a lot from the change in emphasis and language.

There is a lot of new information at this stage. It will help in the movement forward. You can consider the move forward only when you feel both parties have explored all the issues. If this is the case you can consider the movement away from the opening position using the trade stage, as there is no movement in the exchange stage, only clarification.

Trade

This is the stage we all want to reach. It is where real movement occurs and progress towards a satisfactory conclusion is seen. It is too easy to get excited by this stage as you will feel the momentum building. You need to be calm in order to operate in a calculated state and get the best possible deal, not just a quick deal.

There are so many cases where people get carried away by momentum and give away items that they did not need to, as they wanted to complete the deal - just in case the other party became cold to the ideas. Be aware this is not trading as you have gained nothing in return. It is a give-away without strings, which in most cases will be accepted but will rarely lead to a settlement.

I know of a case in a national food company where an experienced Operations Manager gave away an extra two days holiday in order to seal pay negotiations. The person was unaware of the cost or the impact it would have on the company. He was just proud to get the deal. When faced with the costs at a later stage he was staggered that it cost more than the money element of the settlement.

You can make real progress if you get it right and stay calm. It is always best to be tentative at the start of this stage. Let the other party know you are willing to talk about a specific area. You can say "We are prepared to look at an increase of 2% on base rate but recognise this will not match your needs for an increase in holidays. How do you feel about that?"

You have not committed to anything except to look at the increase. You need the other party to comment on the holiday request. This will generate further discussion. You are now able to see what is and what is not important to the other party.

If the approach is rejected, don't be tempted to make a counter offer. Instead, seek clarification of the other party's views and get a detailed response. If you keep changing the offer you will get a set of rejections without any new information.

> I was once given the task of negotiating a change to a production bonus scheme. This was a complex situation, where we had spent a lot of time devising various options that would give a win-win approach for both the employees and the company.
>
> The negotiations were difficult and progress was slow. I tried to get movement by offering goodwill concessions at the end of three different meetings. Each concession was accepted but no further movement was made on the part of the trade union.
>
> Before the fourth meeting my fellow negotiator, the Operations Manager, asked what I would give at the end of this meeting. I asked how he knew that I would do this. He said, "Well, you have done so at the last three, so they will be expecting it again. They are slicing you each week and giving nothing back."
>
> I had not thought of it that way, but he was right. I was all give and building their expectation of more to come at each meeting. I decided not to do it again. At the end of the unproductive meeting the trade union asked, "Where is our goodwill gesture this week?"
>
> When I replied that I was looking for one from them, they looked shocked. They replied, "We never give something without getting something back in return." It was a great lesson, and one I never forgot. Goodwill gestures usually get nothing back and only teach the other party to say 'no', to get even more for nothing. They slice away at your position until you have nothing left.

Another area to be aware of is to look at whatever you are negotiating as a complete package. Don't be tempted to agree to any issues such as base rate on pay and then look at other items of the package. By keeping everything open you can get a better deal. This stops the other party cherry picking the good parts of the deal and rejecting the more difficult aspects.

When making a proposal to move forward, always be positive and sound confident. You need to rehearse what you are going to say so that it flows out and leaves the other person with the impression that it is a positive approach.

The proposal is usually in two parts. The first part is what you want from the other party and the second part is what you will trade for that. The best phrase I was shown by Peter Curren, a great HR practitioner, was "Use the If... Then .... Approach".

Always state what you want from the other party and then state what you will offer. You can say -If you will....... Then I will....... This has impact and makes the other party listen as they know what you want and what they have to offer in return for what they desire. Do it the other way around and the other party often switch off from what you require in return.

Example

If you are prepared to recommend this offer and reduce your holiday entitlement from 30 to 28 days per year, then we will offer a pay increase of 2.5% across all pay grades and increase the shift allowance by the same amount.

Negotiations are about trading what you have for what you want. You give nothing away as a goodwill concession as it can be used later in the negotiations to maybe settle a deal. If it is given away it has no value. We all know that each item has a value to one party or the other.

During this stage you will have shorter meetings than in the earlier stages. You will propose and get some clarification questions. You will then have a longer recess where both parties will consider the situation and review their OMFs. This stage is not completed until you feel you have made significant progress and are near to a deal.

Settle

The final stage is the Settle stage where you obtain an agreement. This is what you have been working towards, so you need to guard against acting too quickly when you feel you have gained an agreement. You can easily make mistakes when you get excited.

Ensure that your settlement fits the three criteria approach adopted at the preparation stage i.e.

> 1. Fair
> 2. Affordable
> 3. Sustainable

By ensuring you meet these three criteria, you are ensuring that the deal is acceptable to the long-term future of the organisation. You will not find yourself in a difficult situation at a later date. You will have been able to persuade the other party that you have been reasonable in your approach and have developed a win/win situation for both parties.

Good practice is to summarise what has been agreed. Do this positively and get the other party to agree to the summary. If there is an error or disagreement, put it right at this stage. You need to get the terms in a written format and read what it says carefully. If you see an error or something you disagree with it is best to verbalise it at that stage.

Methods of Settle

Trial Close

This is where you feel you are there, or near to, an agreement. You state what you believe is agreed and ask for the deal to be put in writing. Only use this when you feel you are very close.

Alternative Close

This is where there are two options on the table. You ask the other person which option they would prefer e.g. A or B. You are saying this as though it is the final act in the process, and need to sound very confident.

Time Limit Offer

This is not used a lot. It is a way of saying the offer is on the table and must be agreed by a certain time. If it is not agreed by the due date it is then removed.

Summary Close

This is the most used close to a negotiation. It is a summary of what is agreed and a request for agreement to the summary. From this summary, if agreed, you go to a written agreement.

Final Offer

This is used when all options have gone. It is a last resort and must mean what it says. If you increase a final offer at a later stage, such an approach will not be believed again.

Good Negotiators

It is useful to look at what good negotiators do in order to be able to copy and use their learned skills. This is how we have developed our skills in other areas of management and our social sports. By observing good practice in action, we can adapt our skills to gain a greater impact on our negotiations.

Most good negotiators have the following approach:

- Keep calm as this keeps the temper in check.
- Use eye contact to ensure points are received by the other party and see any relevant reactions.
- Deliver points with confidence.
- Look confident by maintaining reasonable eye contact (not staring) and use open gestures to show that you are open to views as well as showing confidence in your views.
- Create rapport with the other party by developing a win/win approach and showing you understand the other party's points.
- Don't rise to emotive language or shouting.
- Always show respect to the other party.
- Recognise that it is not what you say but how you say it, and support it with body language that sells a clear message.
- Always summarise progress to ensure the other party sees an issue the same way.
- Use a recess to consider the next course of action for both parties.
- Keep relevant notes to act as a prompt.

This seems to be a credible list of actions. However, you need to concentrate on doing all of these at the same time. It is useful to evaluate yourself against these areas. This will show you what you know you do well and where you need to improve.

It may be useful to get some of your colleagues to evaluate you as well. This will give another side to the process. They may see aspects you have not seen. Always listen carefully to such feedback as it will assist your development. By asking for examples of your behaviour, you will be able to recognise what is being said.

You can use the grid below for the exercise. Score 5 for a key strength and 1 for 'needs a lot of improvement' as before.

Negotiator feedback example:

BEHAVIOUR	SCORE 1-5
Calm Approach	
Eye Contact	
Deliver Confidently	
Look Confident	
Create Rapport	
Don't Rise to Attacks	
Respect Other Party	
Positive Body Language	
Say It Confidently	
Summarise	
Recess	
Relevant Notes	

Now you have evaluated your own situation, you can start to identify how best to make relevant improvements. Consider the impact the improvements will have on the outcome of the negotiations. By agreeing small improvements to these areas you will develop your negotiating skills and get better win/win outcomes.

We have looked at the process of negotiations. This applies not only to pay talks but to any other type of negotiations. You can use the same approach and stages. You need to ensure you are always positive and welcoming.

We now need to look at how you can deal with different types of shop stewards and situations you may face in a negotiation. This will build your skills and boost your confidence when dealing with these situations.

Dealing with Different Types of Shop Stewards

Most people will want to have a successful negotiated settlement to any issue. We all know you can't have your own way all of the time, so we need to compromise. For inexperienced negotiators this is difficult as they see it as losing face. This is usually because they have made a great play with their members about what they intend to do. Sometimes this is fuelled by the members winding up the rep-so coming back from a negotiation with anything less than what they have boasted about is difficult.

You need to help any reps who puts themselves in this position, but not by giving in to them. You need to teach them to manage the expectations of their members in the future so that they will be able to be seen to succeed rather than fail. This is not easy to achieve but you will find it will assist the development of your working relationship.

How to Influence

We all want to influence the people we deal with, both at work and in our social lives. By doing this we tend to get closer to what we want. By applying some simple techniques we can get a better deal, or get there faster. In most cases this will be beneficial to all parties.

We should adapt our communications to the Detail, Task and People approach from the earlier chapters. This ensures your message will engage with the person on the level they respond best. It will also ensure you deliver a message that is designed for the receiver that is more likely to get a positive response.

The phrases you utilise in any communications can assist the influencing of the other person. Some well-known phrases to get the person looking positively at a proposal are:
- I am sure you will agree that…………..
- As you will know…………..
- I agree with your point and I am sure you will accept that I need to make progress with our requirements, which are……..

The above are best said in a positive way whilst at the same time nodding your head. You will be amazed that the receivers will nod their heads at the same time.

When you have a point you disagree with, you can disarm the other party by using the following type of phrases:
- I agree with everything you have said; my only difficulty is……
- I accept 95% of the points you have just made, how can we get over X….(This being a major point, but sounds small because of the 95%).
- Everything you have said makes great sense to me. How can you help me persuade our organisation that this will not increase our costs or manpower?
- Let's assume you are right; how can we get others to accept that this is an acceptable way forward?

The MAP

As with any interface with the trade union, you are trying to build a solid relationship. You need to stay mindful of the MAP as it will show that you need to consider the experience of the other person and the current state of your relationship.

If one party is new to the process they will be guarded about their position, as they will not fully trust you. You need to build trust during the process and be seen to explain what you are proposing, and the consequences of any actions. By explaining you are helping the other party understand the process.

Some organisations will train the negotiating team to ensure they arrive at the negotiations well prepared and able to understand the process they will face. This helps to boost confidence and can generate trust as you have taken the time to train the group.

A natural reaction of a new negotiator is to generate conflict. This may seem natural, based on what they have seen in movies and on TV. You need to ensure this does not occur as such conflict will only lead to poor relations and bad feeling. You can use corridor meetings to overcome any potential conflict.

By having an informal, off-the-record session you can explore any frustrations and explain what you want to achieve. The other party can let off steam if they wish but are more likely to share their frustrations and you may be able to assist in reducing their concerns. Appendix 2 offers more details of corridor meetings.

As the group move forward and upward on the MAP, you will have a more normal type of discussion that will normally be free of frustration and conflict. This only happens when trust is seen to exist between the two parties. Such trust can only be generated over time.

One way to assist both parties to improve is to have a review session after any major negotiation. This should look at what worked well and what needs to improve. If both parties are open and honest, a lot of good progress can be made. The management team needs to take the lead in offering how they believe they could have performed better. This shows that it is not a 'union bashing' event but a positive approach to moving forward.

The final session of the review should look at how the next session of negotiations can improve. Both parties should commit to making adjustments to how they operate. These actions will be agreed and can be used as the starting point of the next session. This helps everyone to improve together. It is a great step towards the conscious confidence we would all like to achieve in our personal MAP.

I worked with one company that had a major difficulty in getting the trade union to accept that they had no further funds for a pay settlement. When the negotiations were concluded they carried out a review session where I was the facilitator.

Both groups talked about the difficulties they faced and what had led to a stalemate at one point. Whilst the groups had not fallen out, they suffered from a lack of trust during the negotiations. The honest review session, which identified some of the constraints both parties faced, helped to rebuild the trust. The openness and honesty of the parties was seen as a positive aspect of their relationship and could be built upon in further meetings. The two groups agreed a number of specific actions they could develop so that the trust was cemented for future meetings. The groups get on well and have kept to the agreed actions.

We have looked mainly at pay negotiations in this chapter. The process described can apply to any type of negotiations. You just need to apply the principles of the POETS approach to the topic. The roles of the team and the preparation are the same in every situation. The main difference is the content.

Let's look at how we will approach the POETS approach and look for any issues. Use the Our Approach exercise to record your views. Outline how you will overcome any difficulties.

Our Approach

Stage	Difficulties	How Overcome
Preparation		
Opening		
Exchange		
Trade		
Settle		

You should now have a plan to overcome any problems. This needs to be reviewed during the negotiations to ensure you stay focused on the process as well as the content.

Key Points

1. Always prepare before you negotiate.
2. Consider the other party's position.
3. Look at the stage of the negotiations using POETS.
4. Ensure your deal is fair, sustainable and affordable.
5. Remain calm during all stages of the process.
6. Give each person a clear role in the process.

Chapter 10:
Discipline and Grievance Handling

Most managers will be faced with a disciplinary or grievance case at least once in their career. In some cases this is a typical happening in their working routine. The handling of these types of issues will form an integral part of the relationship with your shop steward. You need to be able to handle such cases well and be seen to be fair as well as consistent. If you fail to do this effectively you will endanger the relationship you have carefully built with your rep.

Being able to build and maintain your relationship is the key to success with your rep. However, when dealing with discipline and grievance you can often be faced with emotions that can make the relationship strained at times. The shop steward may feel very strongly about a case or may be under pressure from others to deliver a difficult outcome. To overcome this potential problem, you need to be professional and well prepared in order to get the correct outcome for the situation and the consistency of the organisation.

I have been involved with managers who just look at the short term when dealing with these type of issues. In all cases they find that they have greater difficulties further down the line and these have been caused by their own short-term decisions. I can recall one manager who wanted to be seen to be fair as they were new to their role. They reversed three decisions to dismiss employees who were clearly outside the boundaries of their role. The person believed the workforce would see the reversal actions as fair and reasonable and they would respect future decisions. When a person was dismissed for a very serious hygiene issue, the decision was upheld.

Far from respecting the previous decisions, the workforce had now grown to expect a reversal of the original decision based on what they had seen before with other cases. When this did not happen, the workforce went on strike as a protest about the decision being too harsh and inconsistent. This manager could not understand such behaviour. When told by the full-time official that the workforce could not understand the decision in the light of previous decisions, I saw a person who did not know what to do in the future. Had they been consistent in all of the decisions this would never have happened.

So, being fair does not mean being soft or always taking the easy option. You need to consider the impact of your decision as well as how it sits with previous cases. This leads to consistency. You also need to ensure you follow the company agreed procedures, as this will lead to consistency of approach. Giving way to pressure will only lead to poor decision making.

Discipline

All organisations have a view as to what is discipline. In essence, it is maintaining standards of performance and behaviour. Some people will see discipline as a form of punishment due to how the word has been used in the past, say at school. If you are attempting to punish people at work, you are not managing the situation, you are trying to be reactive. When you look at the diagram you will see that it is easy to understand the deviation from the norm of either behaviour or output.

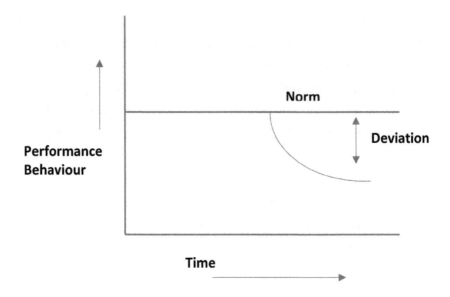

Most organisations look at the disciplinary issue as being either a failure in conduct or capability. The capability is how you perform in the role and conduct is the behaviour you bring to the job.

Looking at the diagram above you will see that you apply your skill and know-how to a job. If any of these are missing the organisation can help you by coaching, training or offering suitable reading. That assistance will be jointly owned in order to make a positive impact on the performance. In this case we are saying that the person can't do the job.

If the conduct i.e. behaviour is an issue, only the person who chooses to use that behaviour can put this right. We all know someone who is good at their job and has a great knowledge of their field of expertise. However, they choose on occasions not to apply themselves to the task in hand. When they apply themselves they are great at their job. When they choose not to apply themselves, they cause problems for all involved. In this case you would tackle the person about their conduct on the job, not their ability to do the job. Too often we get into arguments about the person, as they can do the job so they are immune to discipline. This is not the case if they have chosen not to apply their skill and know- how to a task that they can do, i.e. they won't do it, rather than they can't do it.

You always need to be clear about what you are dealing with, be it conduct or capability. When you are unclear, you will also be unclear of the cause of the issue as well as determining a relevant and practical solution. This can only lead to a poor long-term solution.

I was present at an Employment Tribunal where the HR Director was asked if the issue being discussed in a disciplinary hearing was one of conduct or capability. Their silence was a key embarrassment for all who were there. They clearly had no idea how to answer the question, and as a result the case was weakened severely, as their credibility as an expert was damaged. This is a basic concept, but is so important as it shows whether you understand the nature of the case.

Let us now look at an exercise where you can identify whether a disciplinary issue is either conduct or capability. Look at the exercise and decide where each described issue would fit.

Conduct v Capability

Issue	Conduct/Capability
1. A person refuses to wear safety equipment.	
2. A person makes 10% more rejects than the rest of the team.	
3. A person does not listen to a brief by their line manager.	
4. A person is slow to pick up a new skill.	
5. A person cannot supply their manufactured parts at a quick enough pace for the next part of the process.	
6. A person does not understand the company agreed standards of performance.	

You will see that 1 and 3 are issues of conduct as they relate to the person deciding what they will do. They are choosing their own behaviour and it is deliberate. Only the person involved can change this situation as it is their behaviour that is unacceptable. Only the involved person can change their own behaviour.

The other issues i.e. 2,4,5, and 6 are clearly capability issues. The person is unable to operate at the required level or is less effective than others. This may be due to their lack of experience or lack of skill. The solution will be owned by you and the individual, as you will need to offer a level of assistance that is relevant to the situation. This can be rectified by training or coaching.

As you can see, it is fairly easy to determine the cause of the disciplinary issue. You may find it useful to consider your team and any issues you may have with them. Try to identify if the issue is conduct or capability. Ensure you consider the next step to tackle the issue. You may wish to use diagram to record your findings.

My Team

Name	Issue	Conduct/Capability	My Actions

Don't forget to regularly look at this list to ensure you stay on top of the issues and the situation. It will help you to become more effective and also enhance your team's performance.

Preparation

The key to a good disciplinary case is the preparation. This is true of most management practices. It starts with looking at the procedures that have been agreed for disciplinary cases. You may feel you know the procedure well, but experience has shown me that your confidence increases when you are certain of the procedure. The only way to get such confidence is to read the current procedure. In some cases it may have changed, in others you may be reminded of something you have forgotten.

Always ensure the issue you are considering fits the procedure, and if it does not, then seek out the relevant procedure to which the issue pertains. By using the correct procedure you will know who should be involved in the process and at what level of discipline. Make sure you follow the procedure to ensure you act fairly. If you are unsure of something, ask your manager for guidance. You can be sure a good shop steward will not be reluctant to ask for suitable guidance, so why should you be any different?

At times you may be the person who is to investigate a potential disciplinary issue. This can at first seem difficult. It can be, but only if you use an unstructured approach. Having a clear structure makes the process easier to follow and will ensure a more professional outcome. So where do you start?

You need to get witness statements and talk to anyone who is involved in the case. You need to ensure you have covered all aspects of the case before you decide if you should proceed. It is not a weakness to accept that there is no case to answer. I see this as a strength, providing the facts lead to that conclusion. You need to complete a report to present to whoever asked you to investigate the issue. This report should cover the issues below.

Investigation Report

Compiler   Date................

- What was the initial issue?

- Who else was involved?

- What evidence did you find?

- Who else can verify this evidence?

- What evidence did you find at the scene of the issue?

- What does the procedure say about such issues?

- Has anything like this happened before?

- What action was taken if it has happened before?

- What action do you recommend is taken, and why?

- What should happen as a result of your findings?

Signed………..   Date………..

When you need to proceed you need to make the person aware of the case and offer any supporting documents that are relevant and will help them prepare. The person has a right to be accompanied by a colleague or a shop steward.

Shop Steward

During the preparation you can develop your reputation further with the rep. The amount of involvement will depend on their experience and your current relationship. Where it is a new shop steward you can talk them through what will happen and what their likely role will be if the case goes ahead. You need to ensure the person is aware this is an off the record conversation and is for their development. In that way they will not be surprised when they are asked for assistance. You do not need to share any detail, but you can talk about the procedure and the preparation process. You can also offer help if the case goes ahead.

I well remember a situation at work where the shop steward was being consulted in private about a serious case of fighting at work. This seemed to be a simple case where a very large person (Six feet six tall and 18 stones of muscle) hit a much smaller person for no established reason. It was obvious at this stage that a dismissal was the right course of action.

The shop steward offered a totally different side to the story. He indicated that the big man had been bullied for years by the other person. On at least two occasions the big man had been beaten up outside work by the other person's thug friends. We of course investigated the case and looked at what was suggested and found many witnesses who had heard the bullying and seen the beatings. The case took a totally different turn after the information that was supplied. My lesson was to share with the shop steward as much as I could when investigating, as at times I got a clear agreement on the case, and in a few instances got a new perspective.

You can help new representatives by offering a checklist of issues to cover with their member. This is not exhaustive but will cover most of the issues a new person will require.

Representatives Checklist for Meetings with Staff Members.

Typical Questions To Ask

- What is the person's name?
- What is the persons job title?
- How long have you worked for the company?
- Why do you want my involvement?
- Why is support required?
- What are the facts/details of the issues raised?
- When were the issues first raised with you?
- What is your previous experience of disciplinary or grievance cases?
- How would you describe your relationship with your line manager?
- Have you had a similar experience in another department?

CHECK

- Review the documents received by the staff member
- Review any evidence supplied by the staff member

YOUR ACTIONS

- Explain what support you can offer
- Discuss the likely outcomes of the meeting
- Explain what format the meeting will take
- Explain about the use of a recess/adjournment

With the more experienced reps you can further develop your relationship by explaining what is likely to come their way in the form of requests for assistance. You will be able to give a clear overview and ask for their initial thoughts. This is not horse trading, it is having a respectful relationship. You will be surprised how often the rep offers a set of new ideas or a side to the event you were unaware of, or had not considered. This can only help you in your preparation. Furthermore, it builds a better and stronger relationship.

If you decide there is a case to answer you will be able to develop further contact with the rep. It is best to tell them the case is going ahead and warn them they may be contacted. When a rep is inexperienced you should explain the process of the interview, as well as prepare them to meet their colleague. I always found it worthwhile to warn them to be aware that they may not get the whole truth from the person during their first meeting. There is a tendency to only disclose what is required and offer no more. This can lead to the embarrassment for the rep when the whole truth comes out at the disciplinary meeting.

Talking with a rep before a disciplinary case is not unusual. It can help both parties to explore any anomalies that may crop up in the interview meeting. If you feel you have a very strong case it is worth sharing this to enable the rep to prepare their colleague, but also ensure the rep has been told the truth by their colleague. You should encourage the reps to share why they feel they have a strong case, as on occasions you may not have all the facts. This can prevent embarrassment on both counts. You are not there to win a case, you are there to get a fair and consistent outcome.

I was involved in a case where a shop steward approached me to ask why we were even considering a disciplinary case against their member. The person had no idea they were doing wrong and this was the first time they had been disciplined. The person had stated to the rep that they felt it was not fair as the rest of the team supported their performance and felt they were one of the better operators.

I made the rep aware that this was the third disciplinary case against this person for similar performance and they were already on a written warning. The person's team had formally complained about his work as he was not supplying the parts they needed on time to complete their work. The rep was astounded, as they had been told a lot of fabricated facts that would have made them look foolish if they had defended the person they way they had intended. Whenever a case seems too good to be true, it can be untrue. Share your concerns before the case as it will only help the process.

During a Meeting

The meeting will have a set form as to who goes first and when questions can be answered. It is worth sharing this approach when dealing with discipline for the first time together. When the rep. knows the process, they can deal effectively and knowledgeably with their colleague. This will make the person feel they have had a fair hearing.

Typical Structure of a Disciplinary Meeting

- Greetings
- Introduce all parties
- State the process of the meeting
- Outline your case with facts
- Allow the employee to ask relevant questions
- Ask employee to state their case
- Ask relevant questions
- Summary of facts
- Recess to consider views / facts
- Ask if anything new to add (recess if necessary)
- State what you intend to do

- Offer relevant assistance to improve
- State right of appeal
- Letter to follow to confirm outcome
- Thank all parties

You need to be clear about what you are saying and outline the case in a manner that can be understood by all present. You need to give the person an opportunity to talk and offer their views. What you do not want is for the shop steward to take over the process and answer on their colleague's behalf. This becomes second-hand evidence. You have to insist that the colleague outlines their own case and answers any relevant questions. This at times may be difficult but it is essential. This is not only good for the process, it is good for the shop steward. I have been involved in a few cases where the shop steward has tried to take over the case but has found out part way that they have been given a false story by the person they are supporting. This makes them look anything but professional.

If the case does not go as the colleague expected they will blame the shop steward, especially if they took over the case. By asking the colleague to outline their own case and answer questions, you are protecting the rep from future bad mouthing from the person they were helping. This bad mouthing takes place more than you would believe, especially where the shop steward was not given the full facts prior to the meeting.

It is useful to summarise progress at different stages of the process. This assists the other party to understand what is going on. It is just as useful to get the other party to agree that it is a fair summary. In this way you are making progress together. If they disagree with the summary, ask them why and what needs to be added or removed. This will clarify the situation fairly fast. Never accept a view that they disagree but you do not know why.

You will have another person with you at the meeting. Ensure they take good notes of the event. They can make this more effective by breaking the sheet into two sides: one side for your comments and the other side for the trade union comments. By recording as you go, you get a blow-by-blow account against what was said and by whom.

Typical Example of Notes

Management	Trade Union
AW. Our investigations have shown that PK was absent from 2 Feb until 14 Feb without permission. They did not make Management aware of their return until the day they returned.	
	S.S. There was a good reason for that. PK was in hospital with a broken pelvis.

The Decision

Once the case has been heard and all views have been obtained you need to recess and consider the facts. You should share your thoughts with the person who is sitting in on the case with you, who will be a colleague or a person from Human Resources. You need to spend time deciding what to do and look at what fits the procedure and previous similar cases. When you have made your mind up, ask the other person for their views. Getting them to be devil's advocate is a useful way to fool proof your decision.

When you have reconsidered all the facts you can deliver your outcome to the other party. This should be done with an explanation of why you have decided on the outcome. The person needs to be made aware of their right of appeal and that the decision will be confirmed in writing. It is well worth spending some time summarising your outcome and the reasons for the outcome. This may help if you ever go to an Employment Tribunal. It will show your though process and act as a memory jogger.

DISCIPLINARY DECISION-MAKING SUMMARY

What are the facts?
1.
2.
3.
4.
Evidence of mitigation that were considered
1.
2.
3.
4.
Evidence to support the allegation/issue
1.
2.
3.
4.

Outcome / Decision Made
Rationale for the Decision
1.
2.
3.
4.
5.

There is no reason why you cannot share the contents of this document with the representative after the meeting. It will show how you considered their points as well as how balanced your decision making was when coming to your conclusion. This will help enhance your relationship as you are being open about a decision they had critical involvement in.

A new shop steward may feel they have to appeal the decision. You should have made them aware in the early stages of this process that only the person being disciplined can appeal. Such appeals can be successful but they can also be given a more severe warning. The colleague needs to be aware of that possibility. Always remind the shop steward that there needs to be a clear basis for an appeal. Your appeal should not be around your dislike for the outcome.

I have always found it useful to have an informal talk with the shop steward after a disciplinary case. This may be back at work or in the meeting room. You want to establish how fair and consistent they thought the outcome was, given the circumstances of the case. This can assist the building of the relationship as you can explain why you took a specific course of action. You will also get an insight as to what issues the shop steward was facing. This can only help in the future development of how you work effectively together.

Dismissal

No one wants to be involved in a dismissal as it is in some cases a failure to influence positive behaviour within the workforce. Yet, we need to accept that it will at times be necessary. The outcome of a dismissal can be an Employment Tribunal. This is where you have to show others that you have acted in accordance with the procedures and acted fairly.

To succeed in an employment tribunal, you will need to demonstrate that you have acted as any good employer would. You can only do this by having a positive paper trail that shows what happened. This will include the summary documents above and also the original minutes of the meeting and investigation. You should keep these documents for six months after the person has left the company.

Most people will accept that their dismissal was fair if you have acted correctly during the disciplinary phase. However, the person has 3 months to register their case. They can only register a case if they currently have 2 years' service or more. If the case is a discrimination case, the length of service is immaterial as they have the right not to be discriminated against from their first day of employment.

Grievances

The majority of managers will have been involved in a disciplinary case during their career. The same is not true of grievance cases as they are relatively few in number. In more recent times there has been a marked increase in grievances, mainly due to individuals being more aware of their rights. Therefore, it will be true that a lot of shop stewards will have little or no experience of such cases. In a lot of cases you may be learning together.

Disciplinary and grievance cases are fairly similar in their nature. The main difference is that a disciplinary case is brought by the organisation against an employee because they have transgressed standards of work or behaviour. A grievance is where an employee raises an issue with the organisation or a person in the organisation. The approach to these two areas is fairly similar.

There are specific grievance procedures in all organisations that outline how to raise a case. As a manager you need to be aware of these procedures so that you can hear any relevant case. The initial preparation for the case is completed by the employee, so you cannot prepare until they have raised the case and offered any back-up statements or documentation.

Shop Stewards Grievance

An inexperienced shop steward is likely to ask you for assistance when a grievance has been raised. If they don't, you should seek them out to offer assistance. Be honest if you have not faced such an issue before, as your relationship should be built on truth and honesty. You can learn together. The aim of a grievance is to settle an issue to the satisfaction of the individual and the organisation.

One good question to have in mind throughout the process is, 'What does the party who raised the grievance want in order for the grievance to be settled?' This settlement needs to be realistic, especially since most people who have a grievance raised against them are unaware of the issue until it is raised. It is unrealistic to want the offending party to apologise to everyone in an organisation when the issue is between themselves and one other. In most instances the person only wants the behaviour or issue to cease. Appendix 3 outlines some Dos and Don'ts when dealing with a grievance.

Preparation

As with all things involved in management, your success depends on good preparation. If you do this well, you will get a better outcome. Outlined next is a typical checklist for preparing for a Grievance.

Preparation checklist

1. Ensure the grievance procedure is known by both parties and is followed correctly.

2. The manager hearing the grievance must have played no part in the process or the issue.

3. The grievance is outlined in a letter and clearly states what is wrong, in their view.

4. Any supplied supporting documents are read in advance.

5. The personal file of the individual is examined to gain a full view of their employment.

6. Another manager or HR representative is made available to assist and possibly take notes.

7. There is a private room for the meeting, with no interruptions.

When you are fully prepared for the meeting you need to consider how it will move forward. You will arrange a time and place that suits all parties.

Like all issues, they are best settled as early as possible, so you need there to be little delay in hearing the facts. Most organisations have timescales in their procedures that should be observed.

When conducting the meeting you need to be open-minded about the issue and any facts that are raised. This ensures fairness and clarity in the process. Most meetings will involve a reverse order from a disciplinary meeting i.e. the employee goes first rather than the employer. The process will involve:

- Explain the purpose of the meeting and how it will be conducted.
- Introductions of all parties in the process.
- Allow the employee to outline the reasons for the grievance with details and facts.
- Ask clarifying questions to gain the full facts.
- Ask for back-up evidence to support the issue.
- Explore all the evidence to ensure the full facts emerge.
- Summarise the key areas and get an agreement to the summary.
- Adjourn to consider the facts.
- Be prepared to have time to explore further investigations.
- Inform the employee of the decision and explain why it was made.
- Confirm all decisions in writing after the meeting.
- Ensure the employee has a right of appeal explained.
- Keep good minutes of the meeting.
- Maintain a professional and positive approach.

he approach you take at a grievance needs to be positive and inquisitive. You need to be seeking details and facts but also to be seen as a positive and trustworthy person. Appendix 4 has some typical phrases that are positive and can be used by both the manager and the shop steward.

In most organisations the right of appeal will be based on:

- The procedure was not followed properly.
- New evidence has come to light.
- The decision is unfair, inconsistent or not appropriate in the circumstances.

Any appeals should be heard fairly rapidly but not rushed. This is to ensure the person sees that the organisation is taking their issue seriously. It would be useful to have informal chats with the shop steward during the grievance and appeal stages. This will help both parties keep each other informed of feelings and emotions during the process.

Revenge Grievances

You need to be aware of "revenge grievances". This is where an employee uses the grievance procedure to get back at a person who had disciplined them. So, it is worth assessing in the early stages of a grievance if there is any history between the two parties. If there is and it is an obvious revenge, make the shop steward aware so that they are not caught out by the process.

This does not happen a lot but has been seen more frequently in more recent times. It is sometimes used to put the manager off the disciplinary meeting or to get back at a manager who has disciplined them. Where this is the case, you need to ensure the shop steward does not damage their reputation on such cases. Most management teams will reject such revenge grievances because they are clearly revengeful in nature. However, some cases do get through.

In the worst cases I have seen a person, who is going through a disciplinary hearing, threaten the manager with a grievance if they continue with the case. This can unsettle some weaker managers, but if you let this interfere with your judgement, you will get more grief later. The later grief will come when others take the same step when you discipline them. If it works for one person, others will follow.

If you have an experienced shop steward involved in the case you should try to talk to them before and after the event, to keep a clear view of what is going on throughout the process. They will be able to identify what is a genuine grievance and what is based on false claims. This can help make the process more robust as both parties will have developed a confidence about the real value of the case. Where a case is very strong, your role with the shop steward is to get a lasting solution to the issue that will address the points raised and develop a clear future path for all concerned.

During any grievance case you need to get both parties talking about the issue in a non-guarded manner. This helps get to the real issue and ultimately the best solution. This can be achieved if you work with the rep and share the details of the case openly, so that you both have a similar view of what has gone on in this instance.

I have always found that where you are open and honest with a rep, such behaviour will be reciprocated. It may not come easily at first, but where you are consistent and seem to be trying to get a positive, fair and consistent outcome, the other party will note this and see that it has clear benefits. If you stop trying to do this you will not work together for the good of all concerned.

Where you see both discipline and grievance as a battle and always want to win, you will get the same behaviour from the rep. They will not want to lose and will certainly not want to see you win. The meetings will tend to be more aggressive and confrontational. In this case there are no winners and everyone loses. The consistent approach will turn into a battle which benefits no one in the end.

If you see yourself in this conflict situation, you have to try to develop another approach to rectify the situation. You can only do this by talking to your shop steward about what is happening and what they would prefer to happen. This can be the start of a new era but it will take time to change the current situation. Regular informal chats before and after the cases can help the process develop. Such chats need to be honest and open or they will achieve nothing. Both parties have to work at making a difference. If one fails to respond, you are back to the original position, except the positions are likely to be more entrenched.

Tackle Early

You may not like to be involved in disciplinary and grievance cases, but it is part of your job if you manage people. You cannot avoid these cases, but you can stop the cases getting severe if you take early action with the individual. By tackling issues, rather than ignoring them and hoping they will go away, you can create the correct behaviour and capability in your team. This is what good managers tend to do; they spot any early deviation away from the norm and talk to the individual. This will normally be the end of the issue as the person either was unaware of their actions or was hoping no one had seen what they were doing. Your early action ensures you have helped the person adopt the right approach. If ever the person is involved in a case about this issue, you know that you have tried to put the actions right and the person has chosen to ignore your input.

You need to ensure the person is aware of the deviation and the effect it has on the job or the organisation. By working together you can ensure the person changes their approach and adopts the correct method of behaviour. If you fail to deal with the person, they will rightly believe what they are doing is acceptable. Therefore, it will be more difficult to get them to change their approach as it has become embedded. This makes your job more difficult.

Some managers think it is not worth tackling a minor issue as it may go away or will cause more problems than it solves. You need to look at the lost productivity if you allow such things to continue. Tackling an issue early will save you time later. By pleasantly pointing out an improvement you will motivate a change in the individual. Leaving the issue until the action is embedded, and is the established way of working, will take more time to resolve and take you more time to unravel.

Using the MAP for Disciplinary and Grievance.

The MAP will give you a clear idea about the sort of meetings you are likely to have in both discipline and grievance cases. It will allow you to plan a level of involvement based on the current relationship.

At level 3 you will have a mature professional relationship with the shop steward. This will lead to more adult-type discussions and exchanges during the meetings. Between and after the meetings you will be more likely to share views and help each other to get to a fair solution. This does not mean you will do deals behind the employee's back. What it does mean is that you will share views and information in order to have a more rounded view of the case.

The level of trust at this stage will ensure that both parties will feel free to openly discuss the case without feeling compromised. It will be a given that any discussions will be confidential but useful. The trust will have been built up over time and will assist the relationship.

The reaction you get at stages 1 and 2 will be more difficult to predict as trust is only just being developed. At stage 1 you can get an inexperienced shop steward either being very quiet or being vocal. Both of these reactions can be the result of nerves and lack of experience. It is your role to assist this person in building their confidence in order for them to represent their members more effectively. You can do this before the meeting by explaining what will happen and what you expect of them. This may help put them more at ease.

After the meeting you can debrief the person to ensure they are learning and contributing in the right way. This will assist their growth and make them more effective more quickly. By debriefing at this early stage, you are setting the scene for all future meetings and building your total relationship. This can be particularly handy where a meeting has not gone to plan. By debriefing you can establish what went wrong and why it went wrong. This is good for both parties.

In stage 2 you are starting to build a good relationship but you will get setbacks from time to time. You are both earning each other's trust and it will take time. You will get more adult exchanges in the discipline or grievance meeting, though this can at times be overtaken by emotion. When emotion comes into the equation you get poor results and even worse meetings. It is essential that you look at how to avoid such setbacks in the future. You can use the debriefs for this type of review. If you do not review what you do and how it works, you will struggle to improve both behaviour in the meetings and the approach.

As ever, you need to keep working at the MAP so that it gets you more positive results. Every interaction you have with the person should help you identify how to proceed further towards stage 3. This is not nirvana as you will get setbacks even at this stage, as you are dealing with real issues and human beings, but it is where relationships are more effective.

The next time you face a disciplinary or grievance case don't forget to involve your shop steward. You are in this together and have the same needs to have a secure and effective organisation in the long term. You can learn together and help each other make the workplace better. It may be useful to identify what actions you will take to enhance your relationship when dealing with disciplinary and grievance cases. You can use the exercise to record any relevant actions. Try to keep these as practical as possible so that they can be implemented fairly quickly.

Action Plan Disciplinary and Grievance

My Future Actions	When	Expected Outcome

Now you have completed this action plan, don't just put it away. You need to review this regularly to ensure it is up to date and working. If you are brave you may want to share it with your shop steward. If you explain what you are trying to do and why you are doing it, you may develop a deeper understanding of each other's views and aspirations. It can help where you are trying to get to stage 3 of the MAP and you already have a well-developed relationship.

Key Points

1. Read your procedure before you commence.
2. Involve your shop steward to build their confidence
3. Allow the other party to ask questions and state their case.
4. Discuss the outcome with the shop steward to determine how to act in the future.
5. Take early action to rectify behaviour before it grows into discipline

Chapter 11:
Shop Steward Training

I am sure we all know of a manager who has been newly appointed to a role and receives little or no training. The outcome in their performance in the new role cannot be easily predicted. I am equally sure we know someone who fit this bill and have been a disaster in their new role. This is usually not their fault as they have been let down by the organisation.

Such managers try their best to succeed, but without the correct guidance we are relying on luck. The outcome for the manager can be serious, as they can lose confidence and fail to deliver what is required in the new role. Too often a bad reputation follows the person throughout their career. If only we had spent some time at the commencement of their appointment to recognise what needs to be done to achieve success.

The same is true of shop stewards; they need training to ensure they are successful in their role. Good companies recognise this and ensure this happens quickly, as it helps both parties perform their roles effectively and more quickly.

The majority of shop stewards gain their training from TUC approved suppliers such as Colleges, or direct from their own trade union. Such training will cover what is required from the role and offer various skills to become a good shop steward. The course will usually be day release from work over, say, a five-week period. At the end of the course the person will feel more skilled and confident to do their role correctly. They will still have some reservations until they gain more practical experience.

You need to think about the training the person receives. It can be very good and really focused on the role. However, I have come across some organisations that will question what training was received. A typical quote I recall from one manager was "He went away as a person I could work with and build a solid relationship. He has come back a different person who just wants conflict and is not interested in a working relationship."

This is a sad situation as the manager now has an uphill struggle to get back to the starting position. This can at times be caused by a lack of interest in the training on the part of the company. Another cause can be an overactive trainer who loses sight of the modern approach to employee relations. Whichever it is, you need to ensure this does not happen in the future.

Most shop stewards need to attend training that will cover areas to help them perform their new role with confidence and focus on what is good for the long-term good of their members' employment. This leads to developing good relations with the managers they work alongside.

The training will usually reflect the following areas:
- Roles and responsibilities of the Shop Steward.
- History of the Trade Union movement.
- Overview of current union and future goals.
- Employment legislation relative to the role.
- Effective communications, both verbal and written.
- How to conduct yourself with managers.
- Building effective working relationships.
- Effective meetings with members and management.
- Consultation and what to do at formal meetings with managers.
- Negotiation skills and process.

- Handling Disciplinary and grievance cases.
- Taking effective notes.
- How to carry out the role effectively.

This covers what most people will require. It offers a good base for the person to perform their role at work. If done well it will boost the confidence of the shop stewards when carrying out their duties. It will not turn them into an enemy.

When a shop steward is appointed they will be offered training by their union. This should happen quickly so that they can perform the role effectively and not get into any bad habits. As an employer you need to see the course content and also meet the deliverer. You are allowing the person's release from their duties so you should know what you are paying for.

You should also review how previous people performed after such training in the past. Always ensure you are getting good training for your staff. Seek the views of previous shop stewards to ensure they think the course was useful and relevant to their role in the company.

Once the person is on the course, you need to take an active interest. You need to have a review of progress after each session. This will help you identify if the training is delivering what is required. It can also help you to identify any difficulties the person is experiencing when balancing the role against the trainer's view of the role. You can use the questions below to assist with your discussion.

Discussion questions.
- How did you enjoy your training this week?
- Is the course living up to your expectations?
- What areas did you cover on the course this week?
- How do you intend using this knowledge?
- How relevant is the topic to your role in this organisation?

- Is there anything you need from me to help you with this area?
- What difficulties did you encounter with the content?
- How can I help with that?
- What is the content of the next element of the course?
- Do you need any assistance prior to the next session?

By having regular open chats, you can maintain a good relationship. As a rule, you should have a chat with the shop steward when they are first appointed. This will show your interest and also enable you to establish how the person sees the role. This starts to establish the relationship. It is the line manager's role to enhance this relationship over time. By starting well, you have an easier job in maintaining and developing a good relationship.

The first shop steward I worked with was a positive person. On my appointment to the role, he suggested regular chats to ensure we were both up to date with what was happening in the department. In the early stages I now recognise he was keeping me informed of issues I was unaware of, but he believed would help me in the role.

As the relationship developed, I was able to offer more input. This ensured we built a trust in each other and our views. We also developed mutual respect as we both knew we were helping each other, but no one else was ever aware of how we worked together. I always tried to develop a similar relationship with every shop steward I worked alongside. Sometimes it worked well and with some others it was more difficult. However, the effort was always worth it in the end.

Most good organisations will not leave the shop steward training as a one-off at the start of their role. They will regularly have update workshops and joint management / shop stewards' workshops. These workshops should focus on how to work together or work even better together. If these happen regularly you can usually halt any potential decline in the relationship.

Such workshops are often used when problems arise. This is fine, but it is better to take the initiative when things are going well. It is much easier to look at how to maintain good relations rather than improve them. The most important thing is that a joint approach will be able to set goals and methods of working together to ensure the future is prosperous for all concerned. You can address areas of mutual interest in a positive way that will gain win-win outcomes.

When planning such an event, it is best to involve the shop stewards in the content and planning. It is, after all, their event as well as the management's. This involvement will help to get all the relevant issues out before the event. It will create an element of buy-in to the process that will be missing if not addressed.

When running such events in the past, I have found it useful to follow a format that is positive i.e. will move the relationship forward. The approach needs to include having time to think, both as individuals and as a team. Having mixed management and trade union teams to address areas can give both parties a clear view of how the other party thinks and sees issues; this can only help in future meetings.

You should strive to build even better relations during such events. Getting to know each other better as individuals, not shop stewards and managers, can often open eyes to common backgrounds, hobbies or interests. We tend not to talk about ourselves and our hobbies in employee relations-type meetings as there is a natural business focus. Usually most parties are wanting to get away after such meetings in order to get back to work. So social chat can be limited. We need to get to know who we are working with in order to develop better relationships.

Here is a way to do this at the start of a workshop and get to know each other better. When you know about some-one's hobby or background you can often relate issues to them better, as you can use relevant and understandable examples.

We regularly use a mixture of the following discussion areas as a way to get to know each other better. You interview each other and establish the answers to each area. By having teams of two or three and a mixture of managers and shop stewards, you can develop a good starting point of new knowledge.

Areas to cover:
- What is your employment history?
- Why did you take on the current role?
- What do you like about your job?
- What do you dislike about your job?
- What do you like about the company?
- What motivates you at work?
- What is your proudest moment at work?
- What is your most embarrassing moment at work?
- What is your proudest moment away from work?
- What are your hobbies?
- How do you spend your time away from work?
- What are three things no one in the room knows about you?
- What outcomes do you want from this workshop?
- What is one thing you would change about the company?

The above is a good way to start a workshop. If the team know each other well, you do not need a lot of time on this area and can reduce the questions. Where there are a lot of new people, or they do not see each other regularly, you can spend more time on this. You will be surprised at the level of discussion and the number of people who find they have more in common with others in the group than they thought.

> In one such exercise two people who had never had a good relationship at work found out they had the same hobby. They were both avid steam engine fans and spent most of their time away from work on trains or at engine rallies. From that point on-wards they became much closer and developed a great working relationship at work.

The content of the workshop will vary for all organisations. It will reflect the needs of the time. We need to start such events on a positive note, so it is good advice to look at positive areas first.

Such areas can be:

- What are we doing well at the moment in employee relations, both as managers and shop stewards?

Managers and shop stewards can look at this in separate groups. They can then share their views of themselves and also how they see the other party. There will be some overlap of view which is positive - these need to be praised. The areas which are different can be discussed and remedies agreed, if appropriate.

You can then move onto other areas such as:

- How would you describe the relationship between management and trade union representatives?

Again, this is best done in management and shop stewards groups. It allows free talking and will get an honest answer. The outcome needs to be discussed. Any positives must be looked upon as needing to be maintained or improved. Any areas which are not positive need to be discussed and an agreed forward action applied to get the required improvement.

- How can we improve what we do?

This is another positive approach. It is looking at how to be better going forward. The idea is to look for what needs to improve and then identify what to do to make the improvement. You can run this exercise as mixed groups throughout.

You can also run the first part (what needs to improve) with a trade union team and a separate management team. You will find they have a number of identical issues. When these are explained, both parties can see the other's perspective. The second part can be run with mixed teams to identify how to make the improvement. In this way you will get a better and more robust set of solutions. Where time is tight, you can select a number of mixed teams and allocate one issue each. The teams can present their views to the other groups for amendment or approval.

Other party Involvement

As long as you involve the participants in the planning of these training events, you will identify what needs to be addressed. All parties can input on the content and agree what can be done at each session.

Areas such as disciplinary and grievance trends or consultative meetings are typical of other areas that can be discussed. Where the company is going through major changes, you could include a talk from an organisation who has recently gone through the process. A visit to such an organisation could be part of the workshop.

You need to discuss the content with your shop stewards. After a few years this will become part of the culture of how you operate together. You will have a healthy relationship based on mutual trust. This will be enhanced by ensuring any actions you agree together are adopted. To make this happen you need to spend some time on developing methods of monitoring what is agreed. This monitoring needs both parties' involvement to ensure the correct momentum is applied to gain success.

If you have a workshop every year and the previous workshop actions have not occurred, you will have difficulty persuading the shop stewards of your positive intentions. The process will be seen as just words and no action. By having both parties involved in the monitoring of what actions were agreed you will get joint ownership.

MAP Review

You can use the MAP as a way to review how you are working together as a management / shop steward team. By both parties completing where they believe the relationship to lie, you can identify any gaps. Any low scores need to be discussed and actions identified to rectify.

Any differences in any of the characteristics are worthy of debate. The greater the difference, the more time you need to spend on the debate. By the end of such a session you will have a number of relevant actions that will move you through the MAP towards a better relationship.

This is an exercise that can be developed each year to assist in the movement forward. Even when a team reaches stage 3, they need to identify how to maintain that situation. There are always areas to improve. The achievement of key actions can spur the team on to further actions as the results are clear to see.

Employment Law Updates

Any training provided for shop stewards will have an element of Employment Law. Most people lack confidence in their memory when dealing in this area. Another issue is that the Employment Law is updated twice each year, so a feeling of being outdated can easily occur. Such changes may be minimal at times but none the less they are changes.

Depending at what stage of the MAP you are, it will determine some of the content and all of the approach. With experienced reps you will need more of an update and discussion about the changes. With less experienced reps you will probably concentrate on the main aspects of employment law that are relevant to their roles.

Where conflict exists between the two parties i.e. management and trade unions, a joint course can help to mend bridges and build trust, as they all have the same information. Where a good consensus approach is seen as the norm, you can develop an approach that is discussed and agreed at a formal meeting.

It is a good idea to have at least one update session per year for your shop stewards. This can be run on site and negates the need to go on an external event. The content can be made relevant to the company and the site. By involving the shop stewards, you can identify any area they feel needs to be included.

The employment law update training can involve line managers or be done with shop stewards only. What is important is to show that there is no need to be afraid of the law. By doing this regularly you will enhance the knowledge of the group and grow your relationship. Such sessions offer an opportunity to update, not just on the changes but on areas the group feel are necessary for the current situation, or areas they have forgotten.

The most important element of shop steward training is to ensure it is regular and relevant. If you can do this in- house, you will retain the relevance of the topics and ensure all participants are getting the inputs they want and need. You will not rely on other agencies or the union to keep your shop stewards up to date. You will grow your relationship as you have nothing to hide. It is important to listen to the participants in order to determine what is required to build confidence and knowledge.

It is a useful exercise to try and identify areas where you can train together and develop together. You can use the questionnaire below to identify training needs of both managers and shop stewards. Feel free to add or remove any question. It needs to be relevant to your situation. Honest answers are required in order to get a true reflection on what is required. It is useful to explain what you are doing and why you are doing it prior to issuing the questionnaire. This will remove any lingering concerns that may exist with either party.

Training / Workshop Analysis

1. What area of Employment Law do you feel most comfortable with?

2. What aspect of Employment Law do you need more input with?

3. What areas do we as a company need to improve to build even better relationships with the workforce?

4. What areas of your role do you feel most comfortable with?

5. What aspects of your role do you feel least comfortable with?

6. How can we enhance our meetings together?

7. What aspects of discipline and grievance can be improved?

8. What aspects of working together could we improve?

9. How would you describe the current working relationship?

10. How could we improve how we work together?

By issuing this to managers and shop stewards you can form the basis of a workshop or training event. It needs the participants to offer honest replies in order to get a clear feel for what is required. You may also include areas you feel are important to address. You will get the best results from this process if you share the results openly with all parties. This will show you are genuine in your approach and have nothing to hide.

The programme for the workshop should be jointly agreed, based on the results of the questionnaire. Ideally a structured programme will be the output of the process. This should allow plenty of time to discuss and agree actions. A good facilitator is useful for such an event, especially if the areas being covered are sensitive and difficult to handle.

Any workshop you are involved with needs to have the agreed actions clearly recorded against a realistic time frame. This ensures all parties are able to recall any issues after the event and it prevents any arguments about the agreed actions for each party. You are able to measure any progress by the amount of issues you complete on time, as well as the acceptability of the actions.

When you come to deliver future workshops, you will get a more positive response from all parties if the previous approach was a success. This leads to a better relationship as you are seen to be moving forward together in a proactive manner, rather than being embroiled in conflict.

Whatever success you have with the various workshops, it is worth considering communicating the outcomes to the total workforce. They can see that there is a positive dialogue happening between management and the shop stewards. They will also be able to identify the positive movement that is being made to secure the future of their jobs and the company. The ongoing communication must never be forgotten as this keeps the total workforce up to date. It can alleviate the rumour mill that exists in most organisations. You will be seen to be taking positive steps to keep people informed. This can only be a good thing from the eyes of those who want the best for the organisation.

You need to consider what would happen if you are not proactive in developing your shop stewards. The outcome will vary depending on the people you deal with, but do you want results that will vary? Most organisations will want to be able to predict the results. You can only do this by being proactive and involving the shop stewards in their own development.

Remember that an untrained shop steward will not be able to function correctly, and that is your fault. You cannot complain if they act in a way that is not what you want. You will remain in the first stage of the MAP if your shop stewards do not understand their role in the development of the organisation. This will lead to conflict being an ongoing part of your management role. You need to use your time with these employees to ensure you get the best results for all concerned and spend more of your time on value added inputs rather than firefighting.

Where does this sit on the MAP?

The initial training of the shop stewards is needed so that they can do their job. It helps with the first stage of the MAP. Without the training you will remain in that stage for a long time and may never get any further. The untrained people will only learn off fellow shop stewards, and this may not be up to date or best practice.

The regular updates on key issues such as employment law help this process of keeping the knowledge base up to date. This will assist the growth from stage 1 to 2 as the confidence of the shop stewards will grow.

By having regular and relevant training and maintaining a positive approach you will be developing in stage 1 which can more easily lead to stage 2. Without the training you are more likely to remain in stage 1 and gain a lot of unnecessary conflict. This is bad for both parties.

The workshops will be used to take the teams through the process of stages 2 and 3. The set piece workshops such as employment law updates help you to get from stage 1 to 2. The purpose-made workshops, that everyone has had an input into, will allow the team to develop into and maintain their presence in stage 3.

Without the assistance of these approaches, the team will still develop but at a much slower pace. The reviews and open talking will only happen at meetings where there is an agenda that needs discussing. This is what will hold up the process. If the workshop agenda is about the people and the process of working together, you will make relevant and good progress.

You are familiar with the MAP. There is no reason why you cannot share this with your shop steward at any time. It will show them that the development process is natural and that setbacks can and will happen.

You will be surprised at how well a shop steward will react to such a process. It will help them put their own experience and feelings into a process that is natural. This can help you during conflict as well as when you have a setback. By referring to the MAP you can show that this was only to be expected, as it happens with other teams.

It is worth reviewing what training is required by all parties to ensure you develop a positive relationship. Look at diagram and identify the type of training each person may require. Be as specific as you can and then try to identify a reasonable timescale for the delivery.

What Training?

Who	What	When
Shop Stewards		

Managers		
Total Team		

Now that you have identified the training, talk to the people involved and establish if they agree and require that level of training. Discuss why you believe it will help and talk about the timescales of delivery. This will show that you are looking ahead and want to build a positive relationship.

Key Points

1. Review and discuss the shop steward training at all stages
2. Talk to the shop steward when appointed about their training needs
3. Make training an ongoing topic for your shop stewards
4. Try joint workshops to help move forwards towards stage 3
5. Constantly review training needs for all parties

Chapter 12:
Dealing with Difficult Situations

Introduction

Throughout the book we have aimed to provide you with an underpinning knowledge and understanding to help you build and sustain positive and productive relations with your recognised trade unions and shop stewards.

We have set out a brief historical context of key events that have shaped trade unionism, defined why trade unions exist and given an overview of the legislative framework that trade unions operate within. At the heart of the book is the MAP, a practical framework that describes the key stages of maturity all management and trade union relationships go through.

We have shown you how to use the MAP and given you a range of practical tools and techniques to help you develop your relationships and progress through the MAP. The aim is to progress to stage 3 of the MAP and to have a relationship with your trade union that is based on partnership and founded on the principles of mutual trust, respect and fair and sustainable reward.

We know the route to successful partnership working is not always easy. Stage 1 of the MAP can be particularly challenging to progress through, and it is a stage of development where it is likely that a number of challenges and difficult situations can arise. Remember, it takes willingness, time and sustained effort to build positive trade union relationships. Management must show leadership and take the initiative to drive this process.

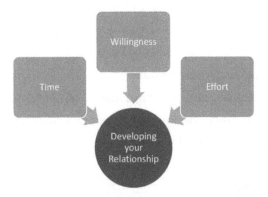

In this chapter we will look in more detail at dealing with difficult situations, why these situations arise and what you can do to resolve them, and ideally avoid them. As we work through the chapter, reflect on the previous chapters and various exercises you have completed.

Difficult Situations

Let us first look at why difficult situations arise in every day management / trade union relations. Have a go at listing below the types of difficult situations you generally experience or that you might run into when working with trade union representatives.

List your examples of difficult situations you typically come across
1.
2.
3.
4.
5.

You will face many difficult situations, but this does not necessarily mean they have to end up in conflict. However, the reality is they so easily can, especially when your relationship with your trade union is at stage 1 of the MAP. You may find it useful to discuss this with someone e.g. your boss or HR manager, who might be able to add extra light on the situation you face, and together help find a way forward.

Difficult situations can arise from a myriad of sources or scenarios. They will vary from organisation to organisation, but in general terms difficult situations are either created by:

- Management
- Government
- The trade union / individual members

However, just because the situation might be difficult, it does not necessarily follow it must be problematic and end up in dispute. Let us look at each of these in a bit more detail.

Situations Created by Management

Businesses must continuously adapt to their changing operational environment. They are constantly having to meet their business targets and increasingly improve their efficiency and/or profitability. Shareholders want a return on their investment and public authorities must deliver value for taxpayers' money.

Managers are at the forefront of delivering these targets and this is a potential source for an array of difficult situations to arise. Most of these situations will affect groups of employees / trade union members e.g. a business restructuring, a proposed redundancy programme, new ways of working, etc. The greater the number of people affected, the greater the risk of the difficult situation escalating into a collective dispute and even industrial action.

On the other hand, managers are also responsible for the application of the organisation's policies and procedures, which ordinarily should be unproblematic. However, the reality is often different, and how managers interpret and apply policy and procedures can be another common source of a difficult situation arising between management and trade unions. This can be due to a difference of interpretation and / or inconsistent application. In the worst case, procedures are ignored.

A common theme we often come across is that managers often spend a disproportionate amount of their time on a very small percentage of individuals. This can be frustrating and lead them to miss a procedural step or try and get to an end result quickly out of frustration and / or competing work pressures. It should be noted that many cases before the Employment Tribunal are found in favour of the claimants (the employee) on the grounds that management failed to follow its own procedures. Working in partnership with the trade union can significantly benefit the manager in successfully resolving these situations.

Many of these policy and procedural issues are in relation to individual cases or incidents e.g. disciplinary cases, individual claims, applications for special leave, etc. It is unusual for these types of situations, difficult as they can be, to end up as a collective dispute, but they can very easily end up in litigation and being pursued through the Employment Tribunal.

Situations Created by Government

Government policy can be another source of potentially difficult situations arising between management and trade unions. A notable example of this has been the sustained public-sector austerity drive over the last ten years, which has forced massive budget cuts across the whole of the public sector. These cuts have necessitated major changes to how services are delivered, the longest ever period of government-imposed public sector pay restraint and thousands of job losses.

Managers have been forced to implement these government-imposed measures and this has created a myriad of difficult situations for managers and trade unions to deal with. Likewise, government-led reforms to public-sector pensions, and fundamental changes to contractual terms and conditions e.g. junior doctors' contracts, have resulted in some of the highest profile strikes since the great General Strike of 1926. What was interesting in some of these disputes was the level of public support. Maybe this is a signal that the scales of power are tipping.

However, these government actions had a much wider impact than just the public sector and because of the cuts, many private sector contractors and suppliers to public bodies were also negatively affected as the cuts permeated through the system.

Even though these complex and difficult situations were not of management's making, they were still left to deal with these incredibly difficult situations with their trade unions.

Situations Created by the Trade Union

Many shop stewards will have you believe all problems are caused by management and are not of their making. To some degree this is true, but trade unions are by no means immune from creating a number of difficult situations of their own e.g. this could be as a result of excessive pay demands, a push for overtime enhancements, extra leave, pursuing equal pay claims, unreasonable resistance to change, etc.

Another source of difficultly I have come across regularly is in relation to facility time (see chapter 3). There is sometimes a lack of understanding by managers as to what facility time shop stewards are entitled to or, more frequently, the issue is how much facility time management think is reasonable, compared to what the shop steward thinks.

Working Positively with Trade Unions

What is often overlooked is that much of the demand on the shop steward is in response to actions from management e.g. to attend meetings arranged by management, representation at disciplinary and grievance hearings, responding to consultation, etc. There is sometimes a negative perception that shop stewards orchestrate time off to do their trade union duties rather than do the job for which they are employed. I have come across these situations, but they tend to be an exception, and once you get the relationship into stages 2 and 3 of the MAP these examples become few and far between.

The table below summarises some of the common reasons why difficult situations arise, within each of these categories, between management and trade unions.

Why Difficult Situations Arise	
Management led	Trade Union led
• Push for increased productivity • Cost reduction • Redundancies • Business / department restructuring • Disciplinary cases • Inconsistent application of policies & procedures	• Restrictive working practices • Resistance to change • Pay demands • Grievances • Facility time • Protecting job security • Equal pay claims
Government led	
• Public-Sector austerity & budget cuts • Public-Sector pay policy • Pension reforms • Changes to employment legislation • Brexit?	

Why Does It Become So Difficult?

It could be argued that dealing with difficult situations is just part and parcel of business life, and yes, it is. The crucial thing is how we deal with them and what impact this has on our management / trade union relationships, and indeed what impact this has on the wider workforce.

The potential for difficult situations to arise between management and the trade union is constantly there. Many of these situations get managed and successfully resolved without incident between management and the trade union.

Therefore, the question must be: Why is it that some managers and shop stewards can successfully resolve difficult situations, whereas others, dealing with a very similar issue, cannot?

Think about your own experiences and list below the reasons why everyday difficult situations that you have to deal with emanate into disagreement between you and the trade union.

Causes of disagreement, conflict and dispute
1.
2.
3.
4.
5.

Having identified these causes of disagreement, you need to consider how you can overcome these or remove the situation in the first place. You do not have all the answers; remember to involve others and seek advice. e.g. HR can bring a different perspective and help find solutions. Ideally you should involve the trade union and agree joint actions.

It's All About the Relationship

Dealing with difficult situations should not necessarily result in dispute and conflict. Of course, some situations can be complex and require some effort to resolve, but lots of managers successfully achieve positive outcomes with the trade union.

Often the crucial difference is the maturity of the manager / shop steward relationship e.g. a relationship at stage 1 of the MAP will be very different to one at stage 3. Those at stage 3 will have a far greater chance of successful resolution and at the heart of this is how the recipe for success is used.

Recipe for Success

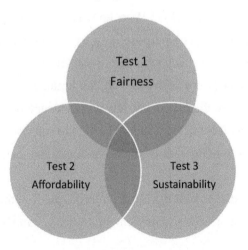

A practical example

Let us take the example of a potentially difficult situation. The trade union have submitted a pay claim for a 10% pay increase; however, inflation is running at 2.9% and the industry sector average increase is 3.5%.

How management react to such a situation is crucial. A typical reaction at stage 1 of the MAP would be to reject this out of all order. But, let us think this through. A core principle of physics is every force has an equal and opposite force, likewise management actions can be met with an equal and opposite reaction. In this example the trade union's reaction can easily become hostile and the dialogue will quickly become adversarial.

At stage 3 of the MAP such a claim would be handled very differently. Using the Recipe for Success above, the manager will sit down with the shop steward or trade union representatives and work through the 3 tests e.g.

Test 1 - Fairness

The manager, despite being surprised by the scale of the claim, will try and understand the basis of the claim, why 10% when inflation is so low, and the industry average is 3.5%? Who knows, the trade union might know something they don't. The purpose is to try and determine, with an open mind and through evidenced argument, whether the claim is fair.

If the manager is not convinced by the argument, he/she will seek to articulate why they think it is not fair and evidence this. Likewise, if the trade union think it is fair they should be able to convince the manager. The important point to remember is this is about rational, evidence based, two-way dialogue.

Acceptance that something is fair, in principle if nothing else, does not mean you have to accept and implement; rather you move to test 2.

Test 2 - Affordability

Let's assume the claim is well founded and considered fair, the question is then: Is it affordable? Management should analyse the financial implications and determine if they have the budget / resources to pay for it or not. It might be the business does not have the money to pay for the award and, if so, this this should be evidential. Simply stating it is unaffordable, a typical response in stage 1 of the MAP, is not going to convince anybody and will only exacerbate the situation.

Relationships at stage 3 of the MAP will likely have an open book approach and share financial data, whereas at stage 1 such information will be withheld, compounding the cycle of mistrust.

Let us assume we have established the claim is fair, but unaffordable. In a positive and constructive relationship this would not be the end of the matter.

The dialogue should then centre on what is affordable or how could it be made affordable. All too often in relationships at stage 1 of the MAP, the trade union expect management to go off and explore the possibilities. Then, when management come back and say it is still not affordable this further compounds the feeling of mistrust and hence the spiral of decline gathers pace.

In successful relationships, management will keep an open mind, and why wouldn't you? They will also involve the trade union in exploring the opportunities and how these might be achieved. Why not think about the art of the possible? Maybe this could be a catalyst for some blue sky thinking and real creativity in terms of a future business model. What's the worst that can happen? It becomes evidentially clear it is not affordable and everyone can see this.

Or it might be affordable, albeit it with various caveats and assumptions. This will most likely lead to some negotiation e.g. if you could do this, we could give this. Remember to think about POETS from chapter 9. The crucial thing to remember at this point is you are not accepting or rejecting the claim, you are engaging in positive, two-way dialogue.

Let us assume, for the purpose of this example, we have determined there is a fair basis for the claim and have determined it is potentially affordable. The third test to consider is sustainability.

Test 3 - Sustainability

It is not in the trade union's or management's best interests to have a short-term solution i.e. that handsomely rewards workers now, only that subsequently goes bust further down the line. The long-term implications need to be carefully thought through and considered.

It might be, for example, that the business has benefited in the last year from a one-off lucrative order, but this will come to an end in two years' time. On the basis of this order the balance sheet might indicate the business could afford the 10% pay increase.

However, once the order is complete and the normal pattern of cash flow resumes, it would not be affordable, plus it would inflate the overheads and jeopardise future contracts and even the sustainability of the business.

Outcome

Therefore, the outcome could be that you agree the claim is fair, potentially affordable, subject to x, y and z, but it is simply not sustainable.

The rational, evidenced-based, collaborative approach based on the Recipe for Success has a far greater likelihood of a positive resolution. The trade union can go back to their members, and you can face your employees, and genuinely say the claim was seriously considered. It is quite likely the process will have identified what is a fair, affordable and sustainable alternative. Such an alternative is unlikely to be rejected, can be jointly communicated to the workforce and have a very good chance of being accepted i.e. a win-win situation.

The Recipe for Success and the 3-test approach can be applied in the majority of difficult situations. This approach is at the heart of the MAP. It is about alignment of expectations and understanding, acknowledging the merits of each other's arguments and working in partnership to jointly resolve issues and agree sustainable solutions, for the mutual benefit of the business and its employees.

The Personality Factor

However, we know rationality can so easily fly out the window. We are dealing with people and with people come emotion, prejudice, bias and a range of other human factors.

One of the biggest factors we see, particularly in stage 1 of the MAP, is personality clashes, power plays and egos getting in the way of rational and constructive dialogue. This is not always easy to overcome and, as we said above, it takes willingness, commitment and time to change this. The reality is the whole relationship with your trade union can come down to just two people i.e. the manager and the shop steward.

Let us take some time to think about personality factors that affect trade union relations in your workplace. List below the personality issues that are getting in the way of the relationship progressing through the MAP.

Personality issues negatively affecting your relationship	How to address these issues

Identifying the negatives in the relationship is the easy bit, the challenge is overcoming these. But if you are willing and prepared to invest time and effort you can overcome these challenges and reap the benefits that a positive relationship with your trade union will bring.

Having identified and acknowledged there are personality factors inhibiting the relationship, we can ask ourselves why these issues are presenting in the way they are. Remember every relationship is a two-way process, or as the saying goes, it takes two to tango. Neither is always right or wrong. The relationship is a series of interactions, and each action triggers a reaction – positive or negative. The secret is to interact in a way that triggers as many positive reactions as possible.

Ask yourself this: how does it feel if you are told to do something, as opposed to being asked to do it, or even better being invited for your view on what should be done, and how? The difference between these approaches is like telling, selling or involving and we know each evokes a very different response.

Tell, Ask or Involve?

The simplest and most powerful way to change the dynamic of the relationship is to tell less and ask more. Ultimately if you have to instruct (tell) then try and frame this in positive terms along the lines of: we need to do this or that, the situation is becoming urgent, and I really need you to do this. What is often challenging to new managers is they generally do not have the authority to tell or instruct the trade union and there is a delicate balance between managing a shop steward in his or her capacity as an employee versus how you engage with them in their capacity as elected shop steward.

The icing on the cake is to say, 'Thanks' or 'I really appreciate this'. If said with sincerity this has a big impact. Of course, you do not have to say thank you to someone for doing what you and they know they have to, but remember when someone says thank you to you, how does it make you feel? It costs nothing and just a subtle change in approach can make a big difference to how people feel. These basic principles equally apply to trade union relationships.

The key to improving the management / trade union relationship is to involve the shop steward. You might think you have the answer, or have determined how you want something done, or what you want to achieve, but if you involve the shop steward in reaching those decisions, this can have far more impact and improve the likelihood of success.

But there must be a sincerity in this involvement. By involving you must be willing to listen and to value their input. Unfortunately, I have witnessed on numerous occasions managers making decisions and then almost as an afterthought saying ' oh, we must pass it by the union' without any real intention of changing their mind. This approach to ticking a box to say you have discussed it with the trade union is soon seen for what it is and will do little to progress you through the MAP or resolve a difficult situation.

There is nothing wrong with starting with a view of what you think should be done, but you must be willing to listen and consider alternative views. None of us have a monopoly on the best ideas. Remember the trade union will be looking through a slightly different lens and this can add real value. I have benefited on numerous occasions from shop stewards bringing to my attention why something wouldn't work. This should not be viewed as a negative thing, it is about positively working together to achieve mutual success.

It is likely when you are dealing with a difficult situation, you are going to have to deal with the shop steward. By involving them, you are engaging them in the process of jointly solving the problem. You open the door to a two-way dialogue and the earlier you can engage the trade union, the better chance of a successful resolution.

Ask yourself: why wouldn't you do this? And is there anything that would change your view on this? List your thoughts in the table below:

Why would you not seek to involve your shop steward?	What would change your stance on this?
1.	1.
2.	2.
3.	3.
4.	4.
5.	5.

It is useful to share this information with others and to discuss how this could operate in the workplace. Maybe discussing this with your boss or HR would help identify solutions.

We Are Who We Are

We are all different and we should embrace and value that difference. People inherently have different personalities and personality traits. We have different styles and approaches to how we like to carry out our duties and fulfil our roles and responsibilities. Some people are introverted, and some are extrovert. Some are quiet, some are loud, some like to jump in head first, and some like to sit back and reflect.

The more you understand your own personality and preferred style of working, the better you are able to understand the strengths and weaknesses of your approach and the impact you have on others. Likewise, the more you understand the personality and traits of your trade union partner(s), the more you will understand the impact that both your own and their style has on the dynamics of the relationship. The key is to recognise that each has its own merits, strengths and weaknesses.

Comparison of Styles

In the table below we have summarised, based on feedback over many years, how managers and shop stewards are typically described by each other.

Types of Trade Union Reps	Types of Manager
1. Table Thumper	1. Assertive
2. Luddite	2. Negative
3. Budding Politician	3. Fair
4. Rabble Rouser	4. Bad-tempered
5. Clever Negotiator	5. Devious
6. Influencer	6. Engaging
7. Skilled Orator	7. Inspirational
8. Moderniser	8. Transformational
9.	9.
10.	10.

- How would the shop steward describe you as a manager?

- How would you describe the shop stewards?

- Feel free to add some of your own descriptors and add these to the table above.

Using the descriptions above it would be easy to conclude that a combination of an aggressive, negative, bad-tempered manager coupled with a table thumping, rabble rousing Luddite shop steward would be unlikely to be a good combination for positive and productive management / trade union relations. But what do such descriptions really mean?

What was interesting in constructing the table above was how there was a tendency to use different descriptors for shop stewards to those for managers. But in reality, are they any different e.g. is the table thumping shop steward really any different to the assertive manager? Is the shop steward who is a skilled orator just the same as the inspirational manager? The reality is managers and shop stewards are just people and, in most cases, trying to do their best.

Often perceptions are formed on limited knowledge or based on isolated incidents. We can be quick to pin stereotypical descriptions on people based on hearsay or canteen gossip. The stereotypes that attract most attention tend to be the negative ones e.g. the Luddite, or bad-tempered manager, and this can significantly affect the development of positive relationships.

However, behind every stereotype is a person, and what I have found on numerous occasions is that when you get to know the person and get to understand them more, their values, their skills, their experiences and qualities, you soon realise that the negative perceptions that have been formed, even cultivated, are often an inaccurate reflection of the real person. The aim is to develop positive management / trade union relationships. The benefits are compelling. Acknowledging the significance of your own personality and that of the shop stewards is a core aspect of stage 2 of the MAP and a crucial aspect of developing positive trade union relationships.

Let us take time to consider what you could do to get to know each other better? List below the actions you can take to do this.

Actions to enhance your mutual understanding of each other
1.
2.
3.
4.
5.

Try to discuss these actions with others to get a wider view. You may even want to share this with the people involved. It will show that you are trying to positively engage all stakeholders in developing the relationship.

There are several simple things you can do to improve your understanding of each other. Make time to meet and talk in less formal environments e.g. a regular coffee meeting just to talk about the general mood of the workplace, and what types of things are bothering people, etc. This might not be comfortable at first if the relationship is stuck in stage 1 of the MAP but work at it.

Completing some personality profiles is a very useful way to enhance your knowledge and understanding. This needs to be done with a qualified facilitator / assessor (internal or external) who can guide you through the process, explain the results and help you interpret these to your relationship and help you identify how you can positively use this enhanced knowledge to move your relationship forward.

Information Is Power

The other most common cause of difficult situations escalating into dispute and conflict between management and trade unions is information, or more accurately misinformation, lack of information and/or interpretation of information.

I have lost count, in my various roles as trade unionist, manager and HR Director, of the number of meetings I have been in where there has been plotting and scheming on what information to share and not share, from either side.

This is indicative of relationships that are operating in stage 1 (Misalignment) of the MAP. The root cause is generally mistrust and one side trying to get the upper hand over the other. As the saying goes, information is power and the belief that if I know something you don't, this will somehow give me an advantage. This may be true in some commercial situations e.g. to gain a competitive advantage over a rival competitor, but this is not conducive to positive trade union relations. You are not in competition with the trade union, the emphasis should be on shared goals and partnership.

I have even seen many times managers or shop stewards leading others to believe they know something the other doesn't. Some might call this a tactic, others might call it kidology. Others might call it disingenuous, or lying.

Take some time to think about the types of information you share, or not, with the trade union in your organisation and complete the table below.

Types of Information	How this is shared with the TU		
	Withheld	Selective release	Openly shared
1.			
2.			
3.			
4.			
5.			
6.			

Critically review why information is not shared or only shared selectively between the business and the trade union, and whether this is helpful or unhelpful to positive and progressive trade relations and successfully resolving difficult situations. Is there anything you could do differently?

There will of course be some special cases where certain information cannot be shared e.g. it might be commercially sensitive, legally privileged or personally sensitive. But, deliberately withholding information, without genuine business reasons, is not conducive to positive and productive management / trade union relations and is likely to thwart your progress through the MAP.

I have seen so many pay negotiations get protracted, unnecessarily drawn out and escalate into dispute because information was not shared, or it was misinterpreted. Likewise, I have seen disciplinary cases get all the way to the Employment Tribunal, only for information to be shared at the very last minute, or even during the hearing, resulting in the case being withdrawn or settled. This beggars the question why could this not have been shared earlier to successfully resolve the situation? A common denominator in these situations is the management / trade union relationship is operating at stage 1 of the MAP.

Successful organisations, operating at stage 3 of the MAP and working in genuine partnership with the trade union, will have an open-book, transparent approach to sharing information. But sharing the information is much more than just handing over documents and data, it is about ensuring there is a shared understanding of what the information means.

Have a quick look at the picture below and jot down what image you see.

Source of image unknown

Most people see either an image of an old lady or a young lady, some see neither and some see both images.

In many respects this image typifies many instances of information sharing when dealing with difficult situations with trade unions e.g. the above picture represents a piece of core information relevant to the situation being dealt with.

In some instances, the picture would not even be shared or disclosed by either side. Sometimes only half of the picture is disclosed e.g. management have the full picture and can see both old and young lady, but only disclose the part of the picture where all the trade union can see is the old lady; but the missing image is key to a successful resolution.

It is not unusual for the information in full or part to be simply handed over, but no explanation of what it means. In this case the other side draws its own inferences on what it sees in the picture. This can lead to information being misinterpreted and lots of wasted time and effort. It is like handing over half a balance sheet or being selective on what data you give, only because it supports your preferred solution.

On some occasions, the information (the picture in this example) is handed over and it is simply taken as understood e.g. it is obvious to me there are two images in the picture, so surely it is to you (can you see the two images?). Or more typically the picture is handed over and the image that management are focused on is the old lady e.g. the old lady is the problem they are trying to resolve. However, the trade union are focused on the young lady. Both images are of a lady, but there is no joint understanding of what image is at the root of the issue they are trying to resolve. It can take several weeks or even months before it becomes clear that both sides, despite looking at the same picture, are looking at different images, by which time the process has become protracted, frustrated and heading for dispute.

The point of this example is to highlight the importance of information sharing AND ensuring clarity of what the information is, why it has been shared and what the information means. It is important to take time to explain and clarify that both sides have the same understanding of the information that is at the core of the situation in question.

It is this information that will provide the foundation of working through the three tests of the Recipe for Success. Take some time to think about how you could improve or enhance the information sharing process between you and the trade union.

Things we could do to improve our information sharing
1.
2.
3.
4.
5.

Once you have identified how you will improve your information sharing, it would be useful to incorporate this into your 5-point plan for success that we discussed in chapter 4.

Information – Consultation – Negotiation

The final aspect we want to cover in this chapter that often affects successful resolution of difficult situations and is another core element of the relationship between management and the trade union is clarity in relation to information, consultation and negotiation processes.

Like the picture of the old lady / young lady above, there can be a lot of misunderstanding in relation to these three simple words. They are terms used in our everyday interaction with trade unions. These terms are often used interchangeably or without due consideration as to what message we are sending out. It is very important to ensure clarity and purpose whenever you use these terms with your trade union partners, as confusion or misunderstanding can easily lead to a difficult situation or make an already difficult situation more difficult to resolve.

What - When - Why

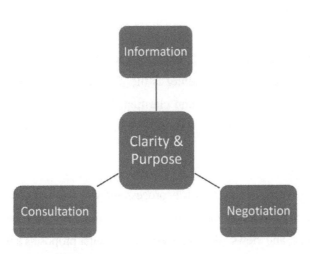

I have heard trade union representatives say on numerous occasions that everything is negotiable. We know this is not the case, but in the absence of clarity of message from management, the default trade union position will be that everything is negotiable.

There are three distinct processes at play:

1. Information Sharing

This is the process of keeping the trade union informed, raising awareness of issues or situations, sharing knowledge and learning, alerting them to emerging and future events, etc. You are putting information out and sharing this in an open and transparent way. It is a key aspect of building trust, helping to ensure everyone is seeing and interpreting the same picture.

This should be a positive and proactive process, ensuring there are no shocks or surprises. Information can be shared in various ways e.g.

- Email
- Newsletter
- Bulletins
- Meetings
- Briefings

There is no 'one size fits all' method, each has its own merits, but in general terms face-to-face briefing is the preferred method as this allows the message to be confirmed and clarified. Providing information, in this context, tends to be a one-way process, although comments can be invited.

2. Consultation

This process is absolutely a two-way process and was covered in more depth in chapter 8. It is a process of meaningful engagement where proposals are shared and explained, and views, ideas, concerns and counter proposals are welcomed.

An essential part of the consultation process is, having received feedback on the proposals, management must seriously consider these and where possible incorporate them. Where this is not possible, this should be discussed in an open and transparent way with the trade union. Meaningful consultation helps achieve the test of fairness in the Recipe for Success.

Unfortunately, in many relationships at stage 1 of the MAP, management will have developed their proposal behind closed doors and pretty much made up their minds already but go through the charade of consulting. This is quickly seen through by the trade union, who then simply take up a position of blocking the proposal. Remember, your actions can be met with an equal and opposite reaction.

Whereas when a relationship is at stage 3 of the MAP, it is much more likely the trade union will have been engaged at an early stage of developing the proposal. There might still be a requirement to formally consult e.g. to evidence legislative compliance and/or wider staff involvement, but this is likely to be positively received. Any new or additional issues that come to light should be genuinely welcomed and considered in partnership with the trade union to see if they are fair, affordable and sustainable.

An important point to note is management do not have to change their proposals, the requirement is to meaningfully consider feedback. Consultation does not require agreement before implementing.

3. Negotiation

Many of the issues you and trade unions have to deal with will require formal negotiation, or collective bargaining. The types of issues will normally be set in your trade union recognition agreement and typically include changes to contractual terms and conditions e.g. pay levels, annual leave, overtime rates, hours of work, etc.

In most negotiations both management and the trade union will determine their most preferred and least preferred options i.e. what they ideally like to get and the minimum they must have. Provided there is an overlap between management's most preferred and the trade union's least preferred options, there is a potential to achieve an agreement.

MPP = Most Preferred Position
LPP = Least Preferred Position

In this example the maximum management could afford to pay is 4.5% and the minimum the trade union will accept without going into dispute is 2.5%. This means there is an overlap of between 2.5% amd 4.5% and we call this the zone of agreement i.e. a deal done within this zone should be acceptable to both sides. Of course, the secret of negotiation is to try and determine what the zone of agreement is and then to try and maximise your position within it.

The better the relationship with the trade union is, it is liklely there will be increasing transparency and understanding, meaning the zone of agreement is readily identified, allowing positive focus on a fair, affordable and sustainable solution.

The POETS model described in chapter 9 will help you achieve successful outcomes from your negotiations.

Importance of Clarity

It may sound obvious, but it is important to be clear with the trade union on each occasion when you are giving them information and for what purpose, when you are consulting them and on what, and when you are wishing to enter into negotiations on what, and why. This helps set expectations from the onset and helps avoid unnecessary confusion as to what process you are applying. To some this is just common sense, which it is, but it is not always common practice.

A time and place for a fresh set of eyes

As your relationship with your trade union develops and you progress through the MAP, the likelihood of you not being able to successfully resolve difficult situations will significantly diminish.

However, situations may occasionally still prove extremely difficult to resolve and potential strains on the relationship can emerge. You may recall from chapter 4 that relationships can sometimes regress and move back to an earlier stage in the MAP. Relationships do not always progress in a simple, linear way and sometimes it can be a bumpy ride.

It is important to recognise the signs when the relationship is becoming strained, which can happen even in the most advanced partnership, and to discuss this openly with the trade union. Sometimes bringing in a fresh set of eyes and getting someone to look at the situation from a different angle can be all it takes to get re-aligned and back on track.

You could ask your HR manager or another line manager to fulfil this role. Similarly, the trade union have access to full-time officers who can bring valuable experience to these situations. Alternatively, you could bring in an external facilitator. ACAS can be an excellent resource to call upon to assist in these types of situations. ACAS have the advantage of being independent and are normally mutually acceptable to both management and the trade union.

Bringing in a fresh set of eyes is not about blame or conceding who is right and wrong. Rather it is about a mature, rational approach and wanting to jointly resolve the situation at hand.

Working Positively with Trade Unions

Take a few moments to think about situations in the past where it might have been helpful to (or where you did) bring in a fresh set of eyes and what this could (did) offer.

Situation	Who could (did) provide the fresh set of eyes?	What could (did) this offer?

Remember, always try and avoid the situation getting personal. Try to keep calm, professional and rationally focused. Try to de-escalate the situation when emotions start to run high. When you spot the signs that the situation is escalating intervene, take the lead and suggest some time-out. Calling an adjournment to a meeting and taking some time-out can be a simple and effective intervention.

When you are working in large groups, try and get some one-to-one time with trusted officials. Sometimes this is referred to as corridor chats and can help de-escalate situations and bring both parties back on track.

Never let the situation fester, be positive, be proactive, focus on the Recipe for Success and where necessary get a fresh set of eyes to help you reach a successful resolution.

What If It All Fails?

If, despite your best endeavours, you are unable to get the shop stewards positively engaged, you need to consider a different course of action. You could:

- Try and rationally discuss with the shop steward the actions you are trying to take.
- Identify which of the three tests of the Recipe for Success you are not agreed on.
- Ask the shop steward what it would take to resolve this situation.
- Ask the shop steward, in a constructive and positive tone, why they are not engaging with you.
- Invite the full-time officer to discuss the situation and see if there is anything they can offer to help move the situation forward.
- Bring in ACAS, either for advice or formal mediation or even arbitration, depending on the situation in deadlock.

If, despite all these efforts, the impasse continues, and you cannot break down the intransigence, you could consider not recognising the shop steward. However, you should not take such action lightly. Be very mindful of the message it will send to the workforce and, despite the facts, how this might be perceived. You could easily galvanise support in favour of the individual and find yourself subject of a formal grievance and / or a potential claim of victimisation on grounds of trade union activity.

My experience is that full-time officers are skilled in avoiding such drastic measures and ACAS offer excellent mediation. It is recommended you fully explore these avenues to help resolve these rare situations and to seek their involvement at the earliest opportunity.

Key Points

1. All management and trade union relationships will encounter difficult situations.
2. Where you fit on the MAP will influence how you resolve these situations.
3. Applying the 3 tests in the Recipe for Success will help you achieve successful resolution to many difficult situations.
4. Understanding each other's personality traits and preferred approach to problem solving is a key aspect of developing positive trade union relations.
5. Don't let situations become personal, try to remain open to suggestions, be objective and rational.
6. Avoid personal prejudice and bias.
7. Make sure everyone is seeing the same picture and there is clarity and understanding of all the necessary information.
8. If you hit an impasse bring in a fresh set of eyes to help you get back on track.
9. Remember the adage, fix the roof when the sun is shining. Don't wait for the difficult situations to arise. Use the MAP and put in place a proactive plan to develop your relationship with your trade union and help your business and employees prosper.
10. Utilise the skills and experience and broader perspective of the full-time trade union officer.

Appendix 1

How to Control Nerves

- Prepare in advance
- Perform a few trial runs of what you will say
- Know your script well
- Tell yourself you will succeed
- Relax the neck and throat
- Relax the stomach / diaphragm
- Take deep breaths
- Take a deep breath before you start
- Learn the first lines
- Remember the receivers want to hear you
- Use a visual aid at the start to take the team's eyes off you

Appendix 2

Corridor Meeting Process

- It is all off the record
- No notes should be taken
- Usually two people from each party
- It is an opportunity to share concerns or explain detail
- Free talking without scripts
- Usually agree the next steps
- Whatever is agreed still needs to be agreed in the full forum
- Used to break deadlock or overcome difficult situations
- It is best to make the other party aware of their use at the start of the process
- Need to gain agreement from the other party to have a corridor meeting
- You can get the agreement to meet either at the end of a session or during recess

Appendix 3

Grievance

Do's	Don'ts
Preparation	
• Ask open questions • Listen • State likely course of action • Outline process • Look at the Policies and Procedures • Record the meeting	• Take over the case • Talk too much • Take sides
At Meeting	
• Ask for clarification • Summarise progress • Listen • Take notes • Ask for recess • Keep calm	• Take over • Tell the person what to do • Get into an argument

Appendix 4

Disciplinary and Grievance Phrases

To Assist the Staff Member Make Their Case
- Could you please expand on that?
- Who else was involved?
- Do you want to add more detail?
- When we talked before, you spoke about X. Could you comment more about that?
- Your manager has stated y. What is your view on that?
- It may help to offer how you felt at that stage

To Assist the Process
- Let me summarise what has been said
- Do you agree with that summary?
- What policy are you referring to?
- What effect does that have on the department / organisation?
- Can we share that data / statement?
- Can we take a recess at this stage?

Involving Phrases
- I am sure you will agree …..
- It is all of our roles to ensure this is sorted
- We must look at what is being said by both parties

- Can you help us with this...?
- We all have the same objective to build a successful business

Appendix 5

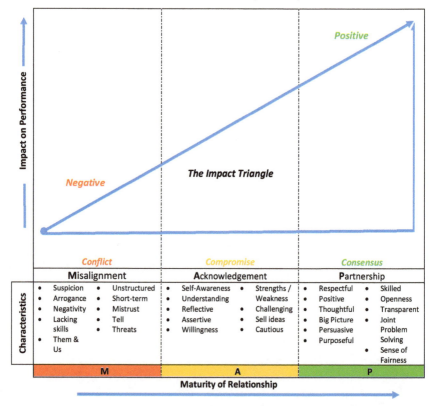

Appendix 6

MAP Questionnaire

How do you rate your Management /Trade Union relationship?	Score out of 10 (1 = low 10 =high)
1. We understand and respect each other's roles.	
2. Both sides have developed skills and use these effectively.	
3. We avoid getting emotive or letting personality get in the way.	
4. We are adult in our approach to dealing with issues.	
5. We are structured and efficient in our dealings with each other.	
6. We are always consciously trying to improve our relationship.	
7. We handle conflict well together.	
8. There is a willingness from both sides to concede and compromise.	
9. We work well together to deliver a positive future for all.	
10. We welcome different views and challenges.	
11. We sell our ideas to each other.	
12. We trust each other.	
13. We always adopt a joint problem-solving approach.	
14. We keep focused on the big picture.	
15. All relevant information is openly shared.	
Total Score	

Appendix 7

How do you rate your Management /Trade Union relationship?	Misalignment					Acknowledgement			Partnership	
	1	2	3	4	5	6	7	8	9	10
1. We understand and respect each other's roles.										
2. Both sides have deveoped skills and use these effectively.										
3. We avoid getting emotive or letting personality get in the way.										
4. We are adult in our approach to dealing with issues.										
5. We are structured and efficient in our dealings with each other.										
6. We are always consciously trying to improve our relationship.										
7. We handle conflict well together.										
8. There is a willingness from both sides to concede and compromise										
9. We work well together to deliver a positive future for all.										

10. We welcome different views and challenges.								
11. We sell our ideas to each other.								
12. We trust each other.								
13. We always adopt a joint problem-solving approach.								
14. We keep focused on the big picture.								
15. All relevant information is openly shared.								

Appendix 8

Appendix 8 - Worked example of group mean score by individual question.

		Score out of ten										
		1	2	3	4	5	6	7	8	9	10	Totals	Group Mean score
Q1	Frequency				2	3	1	3	4	2	1	16	
	Total score	0	0	0	8	15	6	21	32	18	10	110	6.9
Q2	Frequency					3		3	7	2	1	16	
	Total score	0	0	0	0	15	0	21	56	18	10	120	7.5
Q3	Frequency					1	1	5	5	1	3	16	
	Total score	0	0	0	0	5	6	35	40	9	30	125	7.8
Q4	Frequency					1		1	7	3	4	16	
	Total score	0	0	0	0	5	0	7	56	27	40	135	8.4
Q5	Frequency					2	3	1	5	3	2	16	
	Total score	0	0	0	0	10	18	7	40	27	20	122	7.6
Q6	Frequency				2	3	2	2	3	3	1	16	
	Total score	0	0	0	8	15	12	14	24	27	10	110	6.9
Q7	Frequency		1		1	2	3	3	5		1	16	
	Total score	0	2	0	4	10	18	21	40	0	10	105	6.6
Q8	Frequency				1	6	3	1	5			16	
	Total score	0	0	0	4	30	18	7	40	0	0	99	6.2
Q9	Frequency					2	1	4	7	2		16	
	Total score	0	0	0	0	10	6	28	56	18	0	118	7.4
Q10	Frequency					1		7	3	3	2	16	
	Total score	0	0	0	0	5	0	49	24	27	20	125	7.8
Q11	Frequency						5	8	2		1	16	
	Total score	0	0	0	0	0	30	56	16	0	10	112	7.0
Q12	Frequency	1		1	2	5	1	2	2		2	16	
	Total score	1	0	3	8	25	6	14	16	0	20	93	5.8
Q13	Frequency	1		1	2	1	3	3	4	1		16	
	Total score	1	0	3	8	5	18	21	32	9	0	97	6.1
Q14	Frequency					2	1	4	5	4		16	
	Total score	0	0	0	0	10	6	28	40	36	0	120	7.5
Q15	Frequency		1	3		2	3	2		3	2	16	
	Total score	0	2	9	0	10	18	14	0	27	20	100	6.3
All	Frequency	2	2	5	1	34	27	49	64	27	20	240	
	Total Score	2	4	15	40	170	162	343	512	243	200	1691	7.0

This is a real-life example where 16 shop stewards from a large European manufacturing company completed the questionnaire.

Appendix 9

Where I would place my business on the Scales of Power (tick the appropriate box)					
In Equilibrium		In Favour of the Business		In Favour of the Employees	

Actions to improve the balance of power
1..
2.
3.
4.
5.

Which trade unions do you recognise?	Areas of the business covered
1.	1.
2.	2.
3.	3.

Which trade might approach you for recognition rights?	For which areas of the business?
1. 2. 3.	1. 2. 3.

Barriers to Employee Engagement	How Could These Be Overcome
1.	1.
2.	2.
3.	3.
4.	4.
5.	5.

Actions you could take to move from Misalignment to Acknowledgement	What might stop you?	What would help you?

Working Positively with Trade Unions

What action could you take to ensure partnership working is maintained?		
Actions	What might stop you?	What would help you?
1.		
2.		
3.		
4.		
5.		

How do you rate your Management /Trade Union relationship?	Score out of 10 (1 = low 10 =high)
1. We understand and respect each other's roles.	6
2. Both sides have developed skills and use these effectively.	4
3. We avoid getting emotive or letting personality get in the way.	4
4. We are adult in our approach to dealing with issues.	6
5. We are structured and efficient in our dealings with each other.	5

6. We are always consciously trying to improve our relationship.	2
7. We handle conflict well together.	2
8. There is a willingness from both sides to concede and compromise.	4
9. We work well together to deliver a positive future for all.	4
10. We welcome different views and challenges.	4
11. We sell our ideas to each other.	4
12. We trust each other.	3
13. We always adopt a joint problem-solving approach.	3
14. We keep focused on the big picture.	4
15. All relevant information is openly shared.	3
Total Score	58

Working Positively with Trade Unions

	Types of Issues	
	Straightforward	**Complex**
Individual	1. 2. 3. 4.	1. 2. 3. 4.
Collective	1. 2. 3. 4.	1. 2. 3. 4.

Working Positively with Trade Unions

Typical Issues	Who is Involved?		How Effectively are These Issues Managed?	
	Management side	Trade Union side	Good	Could be better
Straightforward issues *Individual:* 1. 2. 3. 4. *Collective:* 1. 2. 3. 4.				
Complex issues *Individual:* 1. 2. 3. 4. *Collective:* 1. 2. 3. 4.				

Working Positively with Trade Unions

Date	What Happened	Resolution	Date Completed

Working Positively with Trade Unions

Relationships

Name	Current Position	Actions to Improve

Styles Evaluation

Name	Delivery Style	Response Style
Self		
1		
2		
3		
4		
5		
6		

Person	Action	When

Working Positively with Trade Unions

Committee Review

What We Do Well	What Needs to Improve	Actions to Improve

What was said?	What did you observe?

Variables	Offer / Response							
	Mgt	Union	Mgt	Union	Mgt	Union	Mgt	Union
Basic Pay								
Overtime								
Holidays								
Pension								
Hours of Work								
Canteen Subsidy								
Safety Wear								
Staff Discounts								

BEHAVIOUR	SCORE 1-5
Calm Approach	
Eye Contact	
Deliver Confidently	
Look Confident	
Create Rapport	
Don't Rise to Attacks	
Respect Other Party	
Positive Body Language	
Say It Confidently	
Summarise	
Recess	
Relevant Notes	

Our Approach

Stage	Difficulties	How Overcome
Preparation		
Opening		

Exchange		
Trade		
Settle		

DISCIPLINARY DECISION-MAKING SUMMARY

What are the facts?
1.
2.
3.
4.

Evidence of mitigation that were considered
1.
2.
3.
4.

Evidence to support the allegation/issue
1.
2.
3.
4.

Working Positively with Trade Unions

Outcome / Decision Made

Rationale for the Decision

1.
2.
3.
4.
5.

Action Plan Disciplinary and Grievance

My Future Actions	When	Expected Outcome

Personality issues negatively affecting your relationship	How to address these issues

Working Positively with Trade Unions

- How would the shop steward describe you as a manager?

- How would you describe the shop stewards?

- Feel free to add some of your own descriptors and add these to the table above.

Appendix 10

Trade Union Quiz – Answers

1. **What historical event proved to be a tipping point for the trade union movement?**
   The Tolpuddle Martyrs, 1833

2. **When were trade unions legalised?**
   Under the new premiership of William Gladstone, the Liberal government passed the Trade Union Act in 1871. This Act legalised trade unions and afforded the full protection of the law to strike. This Act remained in place for over a hundred years and eventually replaced by the Trade Union Act of 1974.

3. **What year was the General Strike?**
   1926 and involved over 1.75 million striking workers who came out in sympathy and support for the million mine workers who had been locked out of their mines in a dispute over a 13% wage reduction and increased working hours.

4. **What did the General Strike achieve?**
   No concessions were achieved for the mine workers. Nine days after it began the TUC called off the strike without a single concession. The miners continued their dispute, but a few months later most had returned to work for less pay and longer hours. Many lost their jobs and remained unemployed for several years.

5. **What is the main reason people join a trade union?**
   For personal representation in discipline and grievance cases.

6. **How many people in employment in the UK are members of a trade union?**

   Approximately 6.6 million.

7. **Which gender is most likely to be a member of a trade union?**

   Women are proportionally more likely to be a member of a trade union. Just over a quarter of all women employees are a member of trade union.

8. **Which occupational group are most likely to join a trade union?**

   People working in professional occupations are more likely to be a member of a trade union.

9. **How many registered trade unions are there?**

   There are 40 registered trade unions with over 6.5 million members. 12 trade unions represent over 90% of all members and just three (Unite, Unison and GMB) represent over 50%.

10. **How many strikes were there in 2016?**

    In 2016 there were 488 industrial dispute strike ballots, 466 of which called for strike action and 436 (94%) resulted in a majority vote in favour of action. 101 ended in actual strike action.

About the Authors

Bernie McCardle

Bernie McCardle has over 30 years' experience of people management and working directly with trade unions. He initially qualified as a road transport engineer then as mechanical and production engineer. He also has master's degrees in Quality Management and Applied Criminology from Cambridge University. He is a qualified Human Resource practitioner and a chartered Fellow of the Chartered Institute of Personnel and Development.

He has extensive experience of working with trade unions across a wide selection of the public sector including public transport, local government and police and prison services. His experience has also extended to working with trade unions in one of Europe's largest car manufacturing companies.

He left school at sixteen and started work as an engineering apprentice for United Automobile Services, one of the largest bus operators in the North East of England at the time. Soon after qualifying he joined the Tyne and Wear Passenger Transport Executive (now NEXUS) to work as a maintenance fitter on the newly opened Metro rapid transport system. He remained with Nexus for 26 years and progressed from the shop floor into management and was promoted to mechanical development engineer. He was then seconded to work with IBM change management consultants to implement a major culture change programme and this led to new career in Human Resource Management and he went on to become HR Director.

As Head of HR in local government he led a major harmonisation of terms and conditions before moving to a newly created role of HR director with Northumbria Police where he remained for eight years. Following early retirement, he has established a successful HR consultancy company and has undertaken numerous assignments including helping lead a major business transformation of the Scottish Prison Service. He has recently been appointed as a non-executive director for one the UKs largest NHS Foundations Trusts.

He was an active trade unionist in his early career and a shop steward for many years. He remained a trade union member throughout his career and he passionately believes in working in partnership with trade unions.

Outside of work Bernie likes to spend time with his family and enjoys playing golf and table tennis.

Tony Weightman

Tony has over thirty years' experience as an HR Consultant and fifteen years as a practitioner with organisations including Procter and Gamble, Unilever and Scottish and Newcastle Breweries. As a consultant he has worked for major organisations both in the UK and abroad. He has worked for Nestle, GSK, Transport for London United Distillers, Nissan and BAT. His work always involves looking at the big picture and delivering practical results.

He has worked on projects as diverse as preparing organisations for crucial negotiations to handling redundancy schemes as well as employment tribunals. He has also acted as an outside grievance handler as well as training managers in the art of practical disciplinary hearings and positive employee relations..

Tony was active in the world of rugby playing competitively for over 35 years. He was President of his local club and has been involved in the recent Rugby world cup. His main hobby at the moment is playing golf without a care about the score. He also likes reading and will always have a good book with him whenever you meet him.

If you have any comments about the book or want to share your experiences of working with trade unions you can contact Bernie or Tony at either Tonyw8@talktalk.net or bernie.mac@tiscali.co.uk

Acknowledgements

Bernie McCardle

Writing this book has been a much greater challenge and rewarding experience than I first anticipated. I could not have achieved this without drawing on support and encouragement of those close to me and reflecting on the many years of experience working with some great managers and trade union officials.

There are four people in my life who have played a monumental role in my personal and career development; my Mam and Dad, my dear wife Susan and brother Glenn who has been a great role model throughout my life. Their unwavering belief in my potential, their support and encouragement to progress and succeed has been a great inspiration to me. I would like to especially thank my wife for her forbearance during many long periods of studying and extended working days and for being there to help me through some particularly stressful times. She keeps me grounded, offers wise counsel and has a great skill of keeping things in perspective. She has been a great support to me during the writing of this book.

I would like to thank my co-author and friend Tony Weightman who has been a great support and mentor to me throughout my career, he is a great motivator, always available to help and has guided me through the process of writing this book.

In work there have been too many people to mention individually who have helped shape my career and form my approach to working positively with trade unions, but I would like to acknowledge three people in particular: John Quinn, Terry McCrady and Steve Culkin.

John was a tough, but fair, engineering manager who appointed me as a maintenance fitter. For several years, we crossed swords when I was a shop steward, but he saw in me a leadership potential and without me knowing it for a while started to test and develop me. John went on to promote me several times, he pushed and challenged me and didn't always make life easy. John played a massive role in my career development and I learnt a lot from him dealing with trade unions. Terry was Director of Finance and Administration and became my boss when I moved into the world of HR. He was one of the most astute, capable and nicest people I have ever worked with. He was a great mentor and greatly helped me make the transition from a young engineer with lots of enthusiasm to a skilled HR practitioner and change agent. I think about these guys regularly.

Steve was Finance director and a chief officer colleague at Northumbria Police. We became good friends and I will always be indebted to Steve's personal support, advice and guidance. Steve and I shared great enthusiasm for transformational change and we shared many similar values in how to treat people and work positively with trade unions.

I have had the privilege of working with many excellent trade union shop stewards and full-time officers who have also helped shape my thinking on trade unionism and they have been part of my inspiration to write this book. These include Gill Hail and Peter Chapman full time officers of Unison, Brian Anderson, full time officer of the Transport & General Workers Union, Caryl Nobbs, Unison branch secretary, Andy Hogg and Phil Ferlie General Secretary and Chairman of the Prison Officers Association (Scotland), Chris Gourley, Charlie Munro and Gordon Armstrong of the Police Federation and Jane Rose, Negotiations Executive with Prospect to name but just a few. These officers are all highly skilled negotiators, people of integrity and advocates of partnership working and have all had an influence in shaping this book.

Tony Weightman

I have enjoyed writing this book with Bernie. He is such an experienced person who is so willing to share that experience. We have developed a great understanding of how each other works. I regard Bernie as a great friend and someone I am always pleased to be meeting.

During my career there have been many people who have made the journey so worthwhile. I regard Peter Curran to be one of the best strategists and readers of a situation I have ever met. He was a pleasure to work for and is a person who taught me so much. The same can be said of Ian Kilgour. It is many years since our paths have crossed but I still regard you as a person who helped me develop and learn about employee relations. You were knowledgeable and fun to be with on any occasion. Both of these were colleagues at Scottish and Newcastle Breweries.

In my early days in HR there were two colleagues at Unilever who stood out. John Harger was my first manager in Cumbria. He was patient but demanding and always there if you were struggling. He passed on his experience willingly. Graham Jagger was also a great inspiration. He never flapped and always could see the big picture. I spent many a night with him and John, widening my horizons. You will never know how much those session helped my career.

In more recent times I have always enjoyed sharing ideas and concepts with Nigel Toon, Jean Cockerill, Adrian Jackson and John Degg. All of these characters have something different to offer. They all share one common feature, they look at the big picture and create practical solutions. All are regarded highly within the organisations they serve.

I would like to thank two very practical employment lawyers from Womble Bond Dickinson who have been a great help over the last 20 years. They have talked at conferences and courses we have run and always delivered what the audience require. The two are James Wilders and Sarah

James who are well known in their field as well as within the local HR community in the North East.

I have worked with many Union officials as well as shop stewards over the years. They have all been positive experiences. The stand out people are Paul Cox the convenor at Nissan, Barry Davies a full time officer from Unite and Tommy Horrocks, a shop steward in Cumbria for what is now Unite. I would like to thank all of the people I have had involvement over the past forty years, you have helped make my life interesting and fun.

Three people have been a great help to me when I was writing the book and probably don't know it. They are well known in their field of music, Mark Knopfler, Eric Clapton and Bruce Springsteen. Their music can act as a stimulator when you most need it and in this case it worked for me.

Finally, my friends in the County on Gosforth High Street who are always available if you need to switch off and talk about something or nothing. They will ensure you are made welcome and get the social interaction you require at the end of a hard day. Unconditional friendship, just like my famous four friends on a Friday night at Northern Rugby Club, Nigel, Phil, Richard and Gareth.

Working Positively with Trade Unions

Working Positively with Trade Unions